JOY

P9-BBV-923

Camilla E. Kimball

Barbara B. Smith

Norma B. Ashton

Elaine Cannon

Anne G. Osborn

Petrea Kelly

Doralee D. Madsen

Winnifred C. Jardine

Claudia L. Bushman

Caroline E. Miner

Darlene B. Curtis

Ardeth Greene Kapp

Emma Lou Thayne

Marilyn Arnold

Nancy Marriott

Lucile C. Reading

JOY

Deseret Book Company
Salt Lake City, Utah
1980

©1980 Deseret Book Company
All rights reserved
Printed in the United States of America

No part of this book may be reproduced in any
form or by any means without permission in writing
from the publisher, Deseret Book Company,
P.O. Box 30178, Salt Lake City, Utah 84130.
Deseret Book is a registered trademark of
Deseret Book Company.

First printing in paperbound edition, April 1989

ISBN 0-87747-819-8 (hardbound ed.)
ISBN 0-87579-212-X (paperbound ed.)

CONTENTS

A WOMAN'S PREPARATION

Camilla Eyring Kimball

As members of The Church of Jesus Christ of Latter-day Saints, we all have common ideals and objectives. The Church is a universal brotherhood and sisterhood. We know the importance of the family and are grateful for the comprehensive programs designed to promote family togetherness. Each of these programs is designed for our happiness and best good.

It's interesting to read some of the comments being made world-wide about the importance of the family to the success of our civilization. I quote:

"Throughout history, nations have been able to survive a multiplicity of disasters, invasions, famines, earthquakes, epidemics, depressions, but they have never been able to survive the disintegration of the family.

"The family is the seedbed of economic skills, money habits, attitudes toward work, and the arts of financial independence. The family is a stronger agency of educational success than the school. The family is a stronger teacher of the religious imagination than the church. . . . *What strengthens the family strengthens society.* . . .

"The role of a father, a mother, and of children . . . is the absolutely critical center of social force. . . . *If things go well with the family, life is worth living; when the family falters, life falls apart."* (Michael Novak, "The Family Out of Favor," *Harper's*, April 1976, pp. 42-43.)

We of the Church have the added knowledge that the family may be the eternal unit of importance if the mar-

This chapter has been adapted from talks given at the Paris Area Conference, July 31, 1976, and the Stockholm Area Conference, August 17, 1974.

riage is sealed for eternity in the holy temple of God. Consequently, this is the objective of all of us. President David O. McKay said that the woman "who rears successfully a family of healthy, beautiful sons and daughters, whose influence will be felt through generations to come, . . . deserves the highest honor that man can give, and the choicest blessings of God." (*Gospel Ideals*, Improvement Era, 1953, pp. 453-54.)

The role of the successful mother is a lifetime of dedication. It is the most exacting and difficult of all professions. Anyone who would say apologetically, "I am only a homemaker," has not fully appreciated the importance and intricacy of her profession. Some of the attributes required to be successful are an unlimited amount of love and patience, unselfishness, and endurance.

A woman should be skilled in child training, in psychology and sociology, in economics and management, in nutrition and nursing. In fact, a well-rounded education will be a great help in caring for and training a family.

There should be love and harmony between husband and wife. In the home is the opportunity for the mother to teach her children to honor and respect their father, who holds the priesthood of God. It is he who will properly preside and direct the activities of the family.

Children should be cherished with the strongest bonds of affection. No sacrifice is too great to protect our families from evil and to rear them in righteousness. Our constant anxiety is that all family members will live worthy of the eternal blessings promised to those who remain faithful to the end. The sanctity of the home must be zealously guarded, for it is here that morality and righteous habits are formed.

Children have an equal responsibility to contribute to the maintenance of this haven of security. There must be complete confidence and trust between parents and children. Obedience of children to parents is essential to peace in the home. Unselfishness on the part of each member of the family is basic to happiness there.

First and foremost, a woman must learn to do intelligent mothering. This is more than highly emotionalized mothering that showers love and affection upon the child and that might lead her to uphold him in wrongdoing. She must realize that the child's future, to a large extent, is measured in her ability to influence and direct him wisely. In the home must be taught faith, self-control, honesty, and loyalty. The gospel of work must be a part of the child's training. There must be provided the environment for the development of the child physically, morally, emotionally, and spiritually. We should constantly hold up the child to his very best efforts.

I should like to quote from the writings of President David O. McKay, whose teachings concerning the family were most effective. He said:

"The most effective way to teach religion in the home is by example, and the most effective teaching of children is living with them. If you would teach faith in God, show faith in him yourself; if you would teach prayer, pray yourself; would you have your children honest, then be honest yourself; would you have them temperate, then you yourself refrain from intemperance; if you would have your child live a life of virtue, or self-control, or good report, then set him a worthy example in all these things. A child brought up under such home environment will be fortified for the doubts, questions, and yearnings that will stir his soul when the real period of religious awakening comes at twelve or fourteen years of age.

"It is at this age that he needs positive teaching regarding God and truth and his relations with others. Activity in the Church is a good safeguard during youth.

Continual absence from Church makes continual absence easy. Other interests in life make the growing youth indifferent to religion. . . .

"There are three fundamental things to which every child is entitled: (1) a respected name, (2) a sense of security, (3) opportunities for development.

"The family gives to the child his name and standing in the community. A child wants his family to be as good as those of his friends. He wants to be able to point with pride to his father, and to feel an inspiration always as he thinks of his mother. It is a mother's duty so to live that her children will associate with her everything that is beautiful, sweet, and pure, and the father should so live that the child, emulating his example, will be a good citizen, and, in the Church, a true Latter-day Saint." (*Treasures of Life,* comp. Clare Middlemiss, Deseret Book Co., 1962, pp. 75, 67.)

I think often of the admonition given to us as parents as found in section 68 of the Doctrine and Covenants, that we should teach our children to pray and to walk uprightly before the Lord. It is for this specific purpose that the Church leaders urge us to observe the Monday family home evening. A weekly home night has been a directive of the Church for many years. We observed it in our home when I was a child. But in these times, when maintaining family unity and compatibility becomes increasingly difficult because of the many distracting interests outside the home that tend to draw the children away, the specific Monday night home evening needs to be considered equal in importance to other instructions that come to us from our Church leaders.

The home evening should be carefully planned, with the circumstances and needs of each family member carefully considered. It should be a happy time, looked forward to by all family members. Gospel teaching should, of course, be a part of every occasion. I have a satisfying memory of the planning and anticipating of our children as we looked forward to this activity together when they were young ones in our home.

Family traditions are important in developing and maintaining family solidarity. When my brothers and sisters get together, which is not often now that we are scattered over long distances, it is still a delight for us to reminisce about our family activities of long ago, when we were at home together. In fact, at one of our family reunions, where there were many of our children and grandchildren, the brothers and sisters reenacted a family home evening of long ago. We recited the simple poems we had said, sang the childhood songs, and had a fun time as we relived our childhood. At one such gathering at our brother's home, he suggested that we sing our father's favorite hymn, "Redeemer of Israel, Our Only Delight." We knew it from memory and sang enthusiastically, thinking particularly of our father. We recalled his characteristics and expressed to each other how much we revere our memory of him. Then we all knelt together and expressed our appreciation to our Heavenly Father for our goodly heritage and for the love that exists in our family. We are none of us under fifty, but we love and respect each other.

I could recount many family traditions, many of which are carrying down to the third and fourth generations in our family. On Christmas Eve we have a special family gathering. It is my pleasure to read the Christmas story as found in Luke, and then the children and grandchildren dramatize the story. The children love to act the parts. One Christmas President Kimball dressed in a costume we had brought from Palestine, representing Joseph, while I dressed in the typical native dress of a Jewish woman, a dress that we had also brought from Jerusalem, and represented Mary. I am sure our grandchildren and great-grandchildren will long remember the story they then acted out of the first Christmas Eve.

When the family comes to the grandparents' home,

we have certain special foods that we know the children are fond of. There are many other special activities that we have found to be particularly effective in bringing each family member into activity.

Sometimes it is possible to turn a difficult problem into an activity that will increase family solidarity. A death of a family member is a time that may have this result. It is a time when hearts are mellowed and love and compassion are brought to the fore. At times like this we comfort and sustain each other.

I would like to tell you of an ideal example of a wedding, which was performed in the Salt Lake Temple. A young returned missionary and his lovely bride were surrounded by grandparents, who were ninety-one and eighty-six years old, whose seven children with their companions were there, some having come from a great distance to be present on this special occasion. The parents of the groom were not there because they were serving in a faraway mission. What greater joy could parents have than to be surrounded by faithful children, who are devoted to the work of the Lord and keeping his commandments?

Holidays should, if possible, be taken together as a family. We had an experience, when our children were young, that necessitated making a difficult medical problem into an occasion for a family holiday. Our youngest son was stricken with polio when he was just three years old. It was necessary to take him to a specialist in a city eight hundred miles away for treatments and operations. We arranged for this to be done in the summer, when the other children were out of school. Each summer for seven years we made this journey by car. We rented a cottage on the seashore, and while Eddie was being treated in the hospital, the other children were with us and had the experience of swimming in the ocean. The important thing was that we were together to share our anxiety and our pleasure.

It would be impossible to make suggestions for individual families, but each of us should be alert to situations that may be utilized for teaching opportunities. Each family has different environment, different interests, different financial situations. But the goal of strengthening and solidifying the family should be an ever-present goal.

The genuine mother takes time to reach beyond her own children and sense her responsibility to help all children. Wherever a child is found cold, hungry, or in need of attention or care of any kind, a good mother will render loving and intelligent service. In the home in which there is an intelligent and spiritually strong mother dwells the greatest single influence on the spiritual and moral strength of the family nurtured there.

I would hope that every girl and woman has the desire and ambition to qualify in two vocations—that of homemaking and that of preparing to earn a living outside the home, if and when the occasion requires. An unmarried woman is always happier if she has a vocation in which she can be socially of service and financially independent. In no case should she be urged to accept an unworthy companion as a means of support. Any married woman may become a widow without warning. Property may vanish as readily as a husband may die. Thus, any woman may be under the necessity of earning her own living and helping to support dependent children. If she has been training for the duties and the emergencies of life that may come to her, she will be much happier and have a greater sense of security.

Another valid reason for a woman to prepare herself to fulfill a vocation is that not all of her lifetime could possibly be completely filled with demands of a family, home, and children. The later years of a woman's life should be viewed as a time that can be socially and professionally productive. When a mother's children are reared, or if she is childless, the years after forty or fifty may begin to look bleak. Her real life's work may seem done, when in reality it has only changed. The active woman cannot hold her hands, so she looks about for something to take up her leisure time. What should it be? Charity? General meddlesomeness? Shall she become a burden or shall she embark upon a new adventure? Happy the woman who has the foresight to see that through forty years of experience, she has matured the ability to commence a grand and useful second half of her life. Let her study a profession or adopt a trade, or find some absorbing subject for study and research. There are many learning opportunities for senior citizens. This is a rare opportunity for advanced study in some subject of special interest. There is no place nor time when one can justify one's self in idly sitting by to vegetate. Keeping mentally, physically, and spiritually growing constantly is the way to continue the happy, useful life.

The Church holds special challenges in temple and missionary work. Genealogical work is also challenging and calls for workers. Family genealogical research is an important and fascinating responsibility, and all families should be anxious that this objective of doing the work in the temple for our dead bring our loved ones into the kingdom of God, so that the family may be bound together for eternity. We know that the family unit is an eternal organization.

If one has a literary talent, active or latent, these are choice years to be productive in this area. Have you written your own autobiography or the biography of a father, mother, or grandparent who did not get this important work done? We all owe it to ourselves, our posterity, and our relatives to leave a written record of our life's activities.

In addition, there are many opportunities for service to others. The world is full of lonely, troubled people who need a helping hand, who need a listening ear or a friendly visit or a comforting letter. Our watchword should be "Never stop growing and serving."

We have talked about the importance of good family relations, about the importance of a woman's education, and about intelligent mothering, or giving ourselves to others in service. Some may ask, "Where can I get help in achieving all of these objectives?" We women of the Church of Jesus Christ are most fortunate to have an organization that has been revealed to a prophet of God and that is designed to help us in achieving and fulfilling all of our basic needs. We have the Relief Society organization specifically for this very purpose. If there are any eligible for membership in this organization who have not taken advantage of it, I would urge that they do so. Its varied programs are designed for our growth and happiness. There is opportunity for participation for each member. It's a wonderful place to make friends and be of service. I would urge each Latter-day Saint woman to be active in this great worldwide sisterhood of the Church now. The visiting teaching program is designed to give us the opportunity to have and be a friend in need. It has been my privilege to have served for more than fifty years as a visiting teacher in the wards in which I have lived, and I find great joy and satisfaction in this opportunity.

The gospel points clearly to the goals that should be continually in our minds as we steadfastly pursue our journey toward our ultimate objective, eternal life with our Heavenly Father and Jesus Christ, our Redeemer. I know of no better directive than that found in the thirteenth Article of Faith, which if we will observe, completely and fully, will help us successfully to reach the destination that we so much desire.

As parents, our great obsession should be to constantly strive to increase our own faith and that of our family members in the importance of the gospel in our lives. The gospel is a way of life. It is a happy way, a peaceful way, a way of joy. A long face and doleful attitude are not prerequisites to a religious life.

We are children of our Heavenly Father; he loves us. I know that Christ died for us that we might return to live eternally with him and the Father. They have outlined the safe way for us to travel so that we may walk to this destiny.

I express my deep gratitude for membership in the Church of Jesus Christ. I express my love for all our sisters, everywhere, and pray that all of us may have the good judgment and the strength of character to keep the commandments, which will assure us, together with our families, the blessings promised, if we are faithful to the end.

Camilla Eyring Kimball was born in Colonia Juarez, Chihuahua, Mexico, a daughter of Edward Christian and Caroline Cottam Romney Eyring. The Eyring family was forced to flee Mexico in the revolution of 1912. She attended Brigham Young University and Utah Agricultural College, then taught school in Utah and Arizona. In November 1917 she was married to Spencer W. Kimball, who in 1973 became twelfth president of the Church. Sister Kimball has been active in the auxiliaries of the Church, particularly the Relief Society.

WHAT IS JOY?

Barbara B. Smith

The young woman gave one last intense push and caught her breath. In the dim half-reality that followed she heard the voices. "The baby is here!" Then for one agonizing second there was no sound, followed at last by a short, tentative cry. She lifted her tired head just enough to see this new child, and reached out her arms. The baby's soft warmth pressed against her, and she knew the task was finished. A sweet, peaceful spirit spread through her soul.

She had brought a baby into the world, and she felt great joy.

What is joy? The dictionary defines it as a strong feeling of pleasure, gladness, happiness. This accurately describes a kind of joy that we know in this life; but joy, as the scriptures define it, is a much more complex concept.

The joy of having the enlightenment of gospel teachings gives a feeling of gladness and well-being, undergirded by a sense of peace, knowledge, and possible achievement that comes with overcoming.

The joy a woman experiences in childbirth is a particularly appropriate example. Jesus perceived it that way too, for he used it to illustrate joy when he explained his own death and resurrection:

"Now Jesus knew that they were desirous to ask him, and said unto them, Do ye inquire among yourselves of that I said, A little while, and ye shall not see me: and again, a little while, and ye shall see me?

"Verily, verily, I say unto you, That ye shall weep and lament, but the world shall rejoice: and ye shall be sorrowful, but your sorrow shall be turned into joy.

"A woman when she is in travail hath sorrow, because her hour is come: but as soon as she is delivered of the child, she remembereth no more the anguish, for joy that a man is born into the world.

"And ye now therefore have sorrow: but I will see you again, and your heart shall rejoice, and your joy no man taketh from you." (John 16:19-22.)

The scriptures give women insight, first, into the nature of joy; second, into the way in which joy is received; and third, into the source of joy. All three are dependent upon each other, and all refer to the hopeful nature of the eternal plan of salvation.

One thing is very clear in a study of joy in the scriptures. It is known to us only as we have practical knowledge of the dark and light of human experience. Others have also observed this aspect of what the word *joy* attempts to describe. The sixteenth-century French essayist Michel E. de Montaigne declared, "The most profound joy has more of gravity than of gaiety in it." The German humorist of the eighteenth century, Jean Paul Richter, observed: "Joys are our wings; sorrows our spurts." And on the other side of the globe the Japanese princess Raden Adjeng Kartini observed, "Those who can not feel pain are not capable, either, of feeling joy."

Women in this dispensation of time, with the restoration of the fulness of the gospel, can come to this profound truth regarding the nature of joy: We need opposites, and there are many. In describing the experience of Adam and Eve, Lehi declared:

"And they would have had no children; wherefore they would have remained in a state of innocence, having no joy, for they knew no misery; doing no good, for they knew no sin.

"But behold, all things have been done in the wisdom of him who knoweth all things.

"Adam fell that men might be; and men are, that they might have joy." (2 Nephi 2:23-25.)

Taking our understanding a little further, the Pearl of

Great Price reveals to us that joy is received as we gain knowledge of our relationship to the eternal plan of salvation.

"And in that day Adam blessed God and was filled, and began to prophesy concerning all the families of the earth, saying: Blessed be the name of God, for because of my transgression my eyes are opened, and in this life I shall have joy, and again in the flesh I shall see God.

"And Eve, his wife, heard all these things and was glad, saying: Were it not for our transgression we never should have had seed, and never should have known good and evil, and the joy of our redemption, and the eternal life which God giveth unto all the obedient." (Moses 5:10-11.)

The significance of observing that the light of joy is intensified by the darkness of sorrow through which a woman plods her way—or, as in the case of childbirth, the peaceful spirit that flows through her following the extreme exertion of childbirth—is that it brings the realization that joy is not easily won.

Joy is not a momentary pleasure. The moments of joy have long-lasting, sustaining power in human lives. It is the nature of joy that it comes after the struggle, both for the individual and for the group. The scriptures tell us that when the people of Israel came together to lay the foundation of the temple after long absence, many "shouted aloud for joy." (Ezra 3:12.)

Also in the nature of joy are feelings of gladness and happiness. In Isaiah 12:3 we read: "Therefore with joy shall ye draw water out of the wells of salvation." And the scriptures repeat often the message of acting with gladness and rejoicing.

The scriptures go beyond these words. They tell us that the source of joy includes the wonder and the peace that come from an understanding of Jesus Christ, his sacrifice, and his great gift to all.

When the angels came to that quiet field near

Bethlehem and saw that the shepherds were afraid, they said: "Fear not: for, behold, I bring you good tidings of great joy, which shall be to all people." (Luke 2:10.)

This is reaffirmed in the book of Mosiah: "Awake, and hear the words which I shall tell thee; for behold, I am come to declare unto you the glad tidings of great joy. For the Lord hath heard thy prayers, and hath judged of thy righteousness, and hath sent me to declare unto thee that thou mayest rejoice; and that thou mayest declare unto thy people, that they may also be filled with joy." (Mosiah 3:3-4.)

These glad tidings prophetically flow from Alma: "Looking forward to that day, thus retaining a remission of their sins; being filled with great joy because of the resurrection of the dead, according to the will and power and deliverance of Jesus Christ from the bands of death." (Alma 4:14.)

In addition to having a knowledge of the nature of joy in the plan of salvation and an understanding of joy because of the great hope of the resurrection of Jesus Christ, we know that joy is a gift of the spirit available to each woman. Throughout the discussion of joy in the scriptures is the recurrent reminder that joy accompanies the Holy Spirit that comes to men and women to bear record of the Lord Jesus Christ. In this way we may know, as promised in the Doctrine and Covenants: "Verily, verily, I say unto you, I will impart unto you of my Spirit, which shall enlighten your mind, which shall fill your soul with joy." (D&C 11:13.)

When King Lamoni, in the Book of Mormon, was under the power of God, "he knew that the dark veil of unbelief was being cast away from his mind," and to him came that "which was the light of the glory of God, which was a marvelous light of his goodness—yea, this light had infused such joy into his soul, the cloud of darkness having been dispelled, and . . . the light of everlasting life was lit up in his soul, yea, he knew that this had overcome his natural frame, and he was carried away in God." (Alma 19:6.)

Paul, in his epistle to the Romans, not only identifies this spirit as the Holy Ghost, but he also helps us know how it can direct our lives: "For the kingdom of God is not meat and drink; but righteousness, and peace, and joy in the Holy Ghost." (Romans 14:17.)

Alma shared his testimony and his powerful conversion that we might be taught by his experience:

"And oh, what joy, and what marvelous light I did behold; yea, my soul was filled with joy as exceeding as was my pain!

"Yea, I say unto you, my son, that there could be nothing so exquisite and so bitter as were my pains. Yea, and again I say unto you, my son, that on the other hand, there can be nothing so exquisite and sweet as was my joy." (Alma 36:20-21.)

The nature of joy is such that this great spiritual blessing can come not alone from one's own knowledge, based on the witness of the Holy Ghost, but it can come also when that blessing of knowledge is shared with others. Each truth that illuminates our souls comes with such power that one can hardly wait to share such knowledge with others. Young missionaries frequently experience this rich outpouring of joy as they serve and teach others.

The fundamental work of the Church has always been to share the gospel, as Joseph Smith told the Saints to do as he left Nauvoo for Carthage: "Minister life and salvation to all mankind."

Alma recorded his joy in sharing his testimony: "This is my glory, that perhaps I may be an instrument in the hands of God to bring some soul to repentance; and this is my joy. And behold, when I see many of my brethren truly penitent, and coming to the Lord their God, then is my soul filled with joy; then do I remember what the Lord has done for me, yea, even that he hath heard my prayer; yea, then do I remember his merciful arm which he extended towards me." (Alma 29:9-10.)

We clearly understand the nature and joy of missionary service as we read: "Wherefore, he that preacheth and he that receiveth, understand one another, and both are edified and rejoice together." (D&C 50:22.)

Alma's teachings enlarge our understanding: "And now, if we do not receive anything for our labors in the church, what doth it profit us to labor in the church save it were to declare the truth, that we may have rejoicings in the joy of our brethren?" (Alma 30:34.)

The Lord's latter-day promise is: "And now, if your joy will be great with one soul that you have brought unto me into the kingdom of my Father, how great will be your joy if you should bring many souls unto me!" (D&C 18:16.)

It is a necessary part of the joy of the gospel that the glad tidings of Jesus Christ and his death and resurrection be shared with others. The joy comes in our personal acceptance of this truth and also in living the commandments. We also experience joy as we watch others achieve the peace which obeying the teachings of Christ brings.

Three scriptures specifically identify character traits we must acquire if we are to know joy.

"Now was not this exceeding joy? Behold, this is joy which none receiveth save it be the truly penitent and humble seeker of happiness." (Alma 27:18.)

"And the angel said unto me: Behold the Lamb of God, yea, even the Son of the Eternal Father! Knowest thou the meaning of the tree which thy father saw?

"And I answered him, saying: Yea, it is the love of God, which sheddeth itself abroad in the hearts of the children of men; wherefore, it is the most desirable above all things.

"And he spake unto me, saying: Yea, and the most joyous to the soul." (1 Nephi 11:21-23.)

"And whoso is found a faithful, a just, and a wise

steward shall enter into the joy of his Lord, and shall inherit eternal life." (D&C 51:19.)

In the Bible, the Lord helps to recognize these traits in the lives of persons who experienced the intensity of joy that comes when a lost soul is found and when a sinner repents.

In the parable of the lost sheep, the humble shepherd left his ninety and nine to faithfully search for the lost sheep. The Lord says: "I say unto you, that likewise joy shall be in heaven over one sinner that repenteth, more than over ninety and nine just persons, which need no repentance." (See Luke 15:3-7.)

He followed this story with the tale of a woman with ten pieces of silver who lost one piece. She searched diligently till she found it, then called all her family and friends to rejoice with her over the one that was found. The Lord told the "publicans and sinners" who had drawn near unto him: "Likewise, I say unto you, there is joy in the presence of the angels of God over one sinner that repenteth." (See Luke 15:8-10.)

In another parable he told them of the love of a certain man who had two sons. One son asked his father for his inheritance and then went into the far country and wasted his substance with riotous living. In dire poverty and feeding swine for a means of staying alive, he thought how the hired servants of his father had more than he had. So he decided he would go home and say to his father, "I have sinned against heaven, and before thee, and am no longer worthy to be called thy son."

However, the father, seeing his son coming, called for the fatted calf and urged all to be grateful and share with him in a feast of rejoicing. He said, "For this my son was dead, and is alive again; he was lost, and is found."

The faithful son was offended, for his father had never killed a fatted calf for him, but the father sought him out and entreated him: "Son, thou art ever with me, and all that I have is thine." This is one joy of the parent.

Another great joy was acknowledged when the father pleaded with the faithful son: "It was meet that we should make merry, and be glad: for this thy brother was dead, and is alive again; and was lost, and is found." (See Luke 15:11-32.)

In his third epistle, John tells Gaius, "I have no greater joy than to hear that my children walk in truth." (3 John 1:4.)

In the human experience of motherhood is another aspect of joy suggested by these parables. A mother may have great joy in the lives of her righteous children while at the same time she may experience pain and sorrow at the wayward and disobedient actions of another child who has not accepted the way of truth.

In the dramatic record of Christ's visit to the Nephites after his death and resurrection, we can feel the remarkable mosaic of meaning that the scriptures give to the word *joy*. The references to joy in the seventeenth chapter of Third Nephi help us to review again this complex, wonderful concept.

First, the need for opposites.

How many thousands of times in the life of a woman is the reality of opposites found and contemplated! I remember so many experiences when this strange, illogical truth has come to my conscious awareness. When my children were young and all at home, I was forced to go to bed for four months to fight hepatitis. In that difficult period of enforced retirement from my daily tasks, I learned that my children whom I had constantly served could, in fact, capably take care of most of their own needs and that they could also give me care that I needed.

Second, the realization that earthly experiences are needed to know joy.

This concept my intellect understands: but life is so fragile and precious. My heart learned this truth one night when my firstborn daughter suddenly stopped breathing. I struggled to force air into her lungs, and when at last she did resume her normal breathing pattern, I knew a joy different from any other I had ever experienced. I then had an appreciation of the fragile nature of mortal life.

On quite another plane of understanding mortal experiences, the value of opposites can be dramatically seen in the physical world in which we live—the rainbow in the clouds, the first bloom of spring after the winter gray. Perhaps the most dramatic example came during the dedication of the monuments to women in Nauvoo. There was a torrential downpour as our first meeting started. The rain came in sheets from the sky and the tent was a haven, but the noise on the tent top was almost deafening. Then, as the prophet stood to speak to the Relief Society sisters assembled, the rain suddenly stopped. He said, "After the rains comes the peace!"

Many of us know that joy follows a struggle to overcome or extend oneself. This understanding is with me continually. I had never had experience in running a large organization when I was called to preside over the Relief Society, a position in which decisions are made and policies shaped that affect more than one and a half million of my sisters throughout the world. Often the struggle is intense to overcome my weaknesses and to meet the needs of so many in such adverse places, but after the struggle come the affirmation and the peaceful joy.

I think of the implicit intertwining of joy with a knowledge of the plan of salvation that came when I met a dear sister in Canada. As she and her family were en route to a church meeting in which her missionary son was to give his homecoming report, there was an automobile accident, and her husband and son were killed. She was left paralyzed from the neck down. When I visited her and asked her how she was, she replied, "Spiritually I'm just fine. I have a good place to live, good care, and wonderful friends I couldn't do without. I know the Lord loves me." And I knew in my heart that she was fine because she understood his concern for her; she had her heart set on eternal perspectives.

Third, the gift of the spiritual affirmation that brings the light of truth and testimony.

I watched this joy come to our son Barton. When he was about fourteen years of age, he went to the Lord with a humble, consistent prayer, asking for confirmation of the gospel truths. He was given a special spiritual witness. It gave us both joy.

Fourth, the comfort of the Holy Ghost's ministrations.

I have experienced this joy often in my calling. On the day I was sustained in Relief Society conference in October 1974, I was spiritually and emotionally strengthened by the words of a hymn that came to me unbidden: "Fear not, I am with thee, O be not dismayed." To know that I had that help with problems, to feel that reassurance, as distinctly as a touch or a sound—how can I describe it? And how could I carry on without it?

Fifth, the sharing of another's growth.

There are many ways in which we find joy in sharing another's growth. I think of a lovely mother who was called to be a Spiritual Living teacher in Relief Society. She worked so hard at this new and unfamiliar assignment, and she learned so much. She shared her experience not only with her class, but also with her family. One day she found that she had terminal cancer. It was her testimony that her spiritual growth, occasioned by the teaching experience, had prepared her and had helped her family accept the inevitable parting.

Sixth, the joy of the blessed state of happiness derived from living the commandments.

This joy expresses itself over and over in personal lives. I think of a friend who recently faced surgery for a brain tumor. As her husband and son were about to give her a blessing, they noticed the anxious concern of her nine-year-old grandson. They turned to him and asked, "Would you like to offer a prayer for grandmother in behalf of all of her grandchildren?" He did. Then they pronounced a priesthood blessing of health upon my friend. Peace and joy were hers. This is the joy that comes to bring courage to meet the unknown quantities of each day.

Seventh, developing the character traits that make a fulness of joy possible.

One night after a concert an admiring fan spoke to one of the world's great violinists and said, "I'd give half my life if I could play like that." The artist heard the comment and said quietly, "Madam, I have given more than half my life to develop my ability."

Developing the character traits that we know are the godlike traits takes a lifetime of practice, but when we have achieved a degree of competence in gaining knowledge and wisdom, expressing love and tender compassion, and in exhibiting self-control, we are close to the joy of achievement that makes life eternal possible.

In the Book of Mormon we read how, after the mighty earthquakes and the great upheavals and the terrible thick darkness, the people heard a voice speak from the heavens. Then, as the darkness abated, Jesus Christ came down and taught them. He saw their faith and asked them to bring their sick, their lame, and their afflicted. He healed them, and all who witnessed and all who were healed rejoiced and appreciated and worshipped him. Then, in the midst of this outpouring, he called for their little children. When they were all kneeling in reverence to him, he knelt with them and prayed unto the Father; and the joy of the occasion is recorded:

"The eye hath never seen, neither hath the ear heard, before, so great and marvelous things as we saw and heard Jesus speak unto the Father;

". . . and no one can conceive of the joy which filled our souls at the time we heard him pray for us unto the Father.

"And it came to pass when Jesus had made an end of

praying unto the Father, he arose; but so great was the joy of the multitude that they were overcome.

"And it came to pass that Jesus spake unto them and bade them arise.

"And they arose from the earth, and he said unto them: Blessed are ye because of your faith. And now behold, my joy is full." (3 Nephi 17:16-20.)

Where the commandments are kept and the fulness of righteousness is allowed to develop, a unique joy comes to the children of men. Such a group achievement has occurred on rare occasions. When it does there is rejoicing and happiness and unity. Isaiah describes it in these joyful words:

"For the Lord shall comfort Zion: he will comfort all her waste places; and he will make her wilderness like Eden, and her desert like the garden of the Lord; joy and gladness shall be found therein, thanksgiving, and the voice of melody." (Isaiah 51:3.)

"For ye shall go out with joy, and be led forth with peace: the mountains and the hills shall break forth before you into singing, and all the trees of the field shall clap their hands." (Isaiah 55:12.)

"Therefore the redeemed of the Lord shall return, and come with singing unto Zion; and everlasting joy shall be upon their head: they shall obtain gladness and joy; and sorrow and mourning shall flee away." (Isaiah 51:11.)

In this day, the Lord spoke to his people and made similar reference: "And it shall come to pass that the righteous shall be gathered out from among all nations, and shall come to Zion, singing with songs of everlasting joy." (D&C 45:71.)

He gave straightforward instruction on how to achieve this righteous state: "If thou shalt ask, thou shalt receive revelation upon revelation, knowledge upon knowledge, that thou mayest know the mysteries and peaceable things—that which bringeth joy, that which bringeth life eternal." (D&C 42:61.)

The record of the saints of the early church confirms what is an absolute in the teachings: "The fruit of the Spirit is love, joy, peace, longsuffering, gentleness, goodness, faith." (Galatians 5:22.)

No discussion of joy would be complete without the realization that joy in mortality is fragmentary. It ebbs and flows where the flesh and the spirit struggle with the temptations and the realities of mortality.

The Doctrine and Covenants should enlighten our search for understanding. Consider these two short statements: "Wherefore, fear not even unto death; for in this world your joy is not full, but in me your joy is full." (D&C 101:36.) "For man is spirit. The elements are eternal, and spirit and element, inseparably connected, receive a fulness of joy; And when separated, man cannot receive a fulness of joy." (D&C 93:33-34.)

The newborn baby brings joy and experiences joy and can give joy through its life on earth, but a fulness of joy cannot be known to the baby or its mother or its father until the spirit and element are inseparably connected in the resurrection and there is an acceptance of the eternal principles of truth that lead to a oneness with Christ himself.

Barbara B. Smith, general president of the Relief Society, serves on the National Advisory Committee for the White House Conference on Families; is chairman of the Child and Family Committee of the National Council of Women; and serves on the American Mothers Committee. She received the Exemplary Woman Award from Ricks College in 1977. She and her husband, Douglas B. Smith, have seven children and twenty-four grandchildren.

THE JOYS
OF TESTIMONY

Norma B. Ashton

His small hands gripped the pulpit so tightly that his knuckles were white. No sound came from his lips. As the seconds ticked on, everyone in the congregation sat silently trying to help this young Navajo Indian boy find the courage to bear his testimony as he had been assigned. Finally, in just a few simple words, he preached a great sermon.

"Brothers and sisters," he said, "my testimony is too small, in the name of Jesus Christ. Amen."

The frightened boy had given us all much to think about. Whose testimony is not too small? Whose testimony can't become larger by sharing it, bearing it, and building it? One of the joys of a testimony is the challenge to keep it living and growing. Through neglect or disuse it will wither and die.

A garden is productive only when it has received tender care and nourishment. Line upon line and precept upon precept we can bring nourishment and growth to our testimonies and make them fruitful. A testimony is necessary for spiritual progress.

Personal awareness of a testimony may come differently to each of us. A young missionary wrote a troubled letter to his father asking why he couldn't have the sudden overwhelming feeling of the truthfulness of the gospel that some converts experience. They can name the day, the hour, and even the minute when the Holy Spirit has witnessed to them that the gospel of Jesus Christ is true. The wise father answered his son's letter by relating to him the following experience, which had taken place as the father began his mission.

Desiring the same kind of sudden impact for which

25

his son now yearned, the father recalled that as a young elder, he had quickly read the Book of Mormon, dropped to his knees, and prayed with real intent to receive a witness of the truth. There was no apparent answer. Again he read the Book of Mormon more deliberately, and again he prayed. Still he felt no sudden impact or direct answer. The process was repeated a third time. As he was praying to the Lord, the father reported that a peaceful feeling came over him and this thought penetrated his consciousness: "You have always known that the gospel is true; you have a testimony. Now get up and go to work. Feed that testimony, nourish it, and share it."

Later the missionary son told his father how much the relating of that experience had helped him. He too decided that his testimony had always been with him, and that he too must go to work to expand and build upon what he already possessed.

This father and son call their testimonies the quiet kind—the kind that comes line upon line, precept upon precept, until the testimony is deep and strong.

Both the sudden impact testimony and the quiet testimony are good. Neither is better than the other. Both kinds must be constantly used and nourished in order to know the joy of having a testimony.

The more dramatic experiences in acquiring a testimony are actually rare. Often the realization that we do have a testimony comes as we look at our lives in retrospect and see God's hand in the blessings that have come to us. There should be no feeling of inadequacy if our testimonies creep quietly into our lives instead of bursting in like a shooting star.

As doctors tell us about the muscles of our body—"Use them or lose them"—so it is with testimonies. To give only lip service to a testimony is hypocritical. Joy comes from having such a strong internalized belief in the truths taught by our Savior that we are moved to action.

Of course, bearing a testimony is more than lip

service as long as our deeds match our words. But to bear testimony and then in daily acts ignore the teachings of our Savior makes a mockery of the words spoken.

A Testimony Brings Growth

In Tokyo a young lady was converted and baptized into the Church. Her testimony grew and so did she, as she lived the principles of the gospel and fulfilled her assignments in the Church. Although her mother did not choose to change her religious affiliation, she liked what was happening to her daughter. One day the mother went to the mission home and made this statement to the elders, "I like what your church is doing for my daughter. I wish you would baptize my son. But you will have to hold him under the water longer because he needs to change more than his sister did." Of course, work, not water, helps people and testimonies grow. "Faith, if it hath not works, is dead." (James 2:17.)

A testimony guides our efforts to pathways that can lead to growth and joy. God does not choose to force us to obey his commandments. He merely gives us a clear explanation of his laws and reveals the blessings that can be realized through obedience. Never does God take from us our freedom to choose. He may say "I forbid it," but he also tells us that we may choose. "But of the tree of knowledge of good and evil, thou shalt not eat of it, nevertheless, thou mayest choose for thyself, for it is given unto thee; but, remember that I forbid it." (Moses 3:17.) Our agency is never withdrawn. However, we may lose our ability to choose if we so fetter ourselves with bad habits or wrong actions that we lose self-control and fall into Satan's power.

With a testimony, right paths are easier to find and to follow. Uncertainty about proper actions is alleviated when we can ask, "Is this what Jesus would have me do?" If the answer is not immediately evident, a prayerful search of the scriptures usually points the way.

Someone has said, "There are no secrets of success.

27

Success is doing the things you should do. Success is not doing the things you should not do." In order to be free to do those things we want to do, we have to determine those things we will not do. Robert Louis Stevenson wrote, "Saints are sinners who kept on trying." We do need a game plan so we will not run wildly around in circles. A testimony can be a guide in forming our game plan; it gives a solid foundation of correct principles on which to base our day-to-day actions.

For many of us time is limiting. There are many things in life in which we have an interest, but we cannot implement them all. Our testimonies can aid in selection of priorities.

Most of us have been given assignments in the Church that we have believed we were not capable of fulfilling properly. With fear and doubt we have gone to our knees and prayed for help. To our amazement we have been able to do a creditable job. Our Father in heaven has helped us. After several such experiences we become aware of the fact that we have more potential than we suspect when we can turn to God for assistance. He has more confidence in us than we know. We can surprise everyone, including ourselves, if we will let ourselves grow with the gospel. Our testimony becomes a motivating force for action, and we realize the joy that comes from achievement.

A Testimony Gives Direction

"Choose you this day whom ye will serve . . . but as for me and my house, we will serve the Lord." (Joshua 24:15.)

There is a hue and cry in the world today to be yourself, find yourself, know yourself, do your own thing. Voices of every kind call from every side. Each of us must examine facts and philosophies of the world with an open mind, but also with a prayer for guidance as we make choices and set goals. One must ask, "What is my con-

cept of life? What forces will guide me? What will I reject? To what will I yield?" Without deep introspection,
no testimony is viable. Every person in the Church
should examine his beliefs and actions in relation to the
basic principles of the gospel.

President Heber C. Kimball once said, "To meet the
difficulties that are coming, it will be necessary for you to
have a knowledge of the truth of this work for
yourselves. . . . If you have not got the testimony, live
right and call upon the Lord and cease not till you obtain
it. If you do not you will not stand.

"Remember these sayings, for many of you will live to
see them fulfilled. The time will come when no man nor
woman will be able to endure on borrowed light. Each
will have to be guided by the light within himself. If you
do not have it, how can you stand? Do you believe it?"
(Orson F. Whitney, *Life of Heber C. Kimball*, Bookcraft,
1979, p. 450.)

If we don't plan and stay in control of our lives, un-
planned circumstances may run our lives.

To make right choices and set worthwhile goals, we
need to be able to evaluate the evidence not only in relationship to the present, but also in perspective for the future. Too often immediate demands of the day block out
an awareness of the needs we may encounter tomorrow.
Like the foolish virgins, we may postpone the purchase of
oil for our lamps until it is too late.

If we had to systematically weigh all the known evidence relating to each decision or action facing us, our
lives would move slowly and laboriously. Our time and
energy are limited. There are many paths to travel, many
forks in the road, many interesting activities in which to
participate. Which paths shall we tread, which direction
should we take? We may ask as did Saul of Tarsus when
he was on the way to Damascus, "Lord, what wilt thou
have me do?" (Acts 9:6.)

A testimony can be our own personal Liahona, a

guiding force in our lives. In an atmosphere of pressure and wonderment it may be the only thing strong enough to help us look past the present moment and plan the future in the framework of the gospel.

A testimony can expedite decision making because it gives specific guidelines concerning what we should and should not do. When blatant voices vie for our support, it gives us the strength to follow the advice given by Henry Van Dyke: "You may have to live in a crowd, but you don't have to live like it."

Each act and decision matters because we are eternal beings.

A Testimony Brings Security

How often have we heard, "Follow the prophet; he will never lead you astray"? Those with a strong testimony have tried this counsel and not found it wanting. How can we develop a testimony strong enough to follow the prophets?

A young mother was watching her five-year-old son play a soccer game. With surefootedness he ran up and down the playing field following the ball. He could kick the ball with one leg and never fall. On the grass near the sidelines, his one-year-old brother was carefully learning to take one faltering step after another. Even holding mother's fingers, he tumbled to the grass occasionally. Soon an older brother came down the sidewalk, almost flying on his skateboard. With complete confidence he drew up by his mother and jumped off his skateboard. Three boys, three sets of legs, each at a different stage of development. Why the difference? Could it be experience, practice, and confidence?

First the boys learned to stand. Next came walking and surefooted running. With practice and effort, balance and speed became second nature to the oldest son. So it is as we learn to follow the prophets. We listen, ponder, and then put the counsel to a test. As we practice, it becomes easier to walk with our leaders. Finally experience teaches us that balance and security can be ours if we follow our prophet.

None of us can develop expertise in every field. We turn to doctors during illness, to plumbers when a pipe breaks in the sprinkling system, and to professors to help us get college degrees. Nor can we know all there is to know about the gospel. Our vision is limited. This is added security when we know that we have a living prophet, seer, and revelator whom we can trust; who will never be permitted to lead us astray; who will be a constant resource for correct guidance.

With a testimony comes the joy of knowing that "I am a child of God." We can become creative and productive. We can face the future with anticipation and joy knowing that with God's help we can do all things.

As challenges come, we learn through pain and struggle that we are more than we thought we were. We understand what the Lord meant when he gave us this great truth: "I, the Lord, am bound when ye do what I say; but when ye do not what I say, ye have no promise." (D&C 82:10.) Tests help us stretch and grow as we seek solutions. A testimony gives us power to rise to our potential because we understand that God has faith in us. It can give us a burst of confidence about ourselves and about the future.

A Testimony Brings Peace

Oliver Wendell Holmes was only about five feet tall. In a large meeting he was the shortest person in attendance. A man said to him, "Don't you feel strange being so short among all these taller men?" "Yes," Mr. Holmes replied, "I feel like a dime among pennies." He was at peace with his situation.

In a world of challenges there are many things to make us feel strange, many things to threaten our self-image. At such times a testimony can fortify us. The

31

scriptures reassure us time after time that God is our Father and he is at our side waiting to help us with life's assignments.

It is comforting to read in Matthew 19:26, "With men this is impossible; but with God all things are possible."

A testimony gives peace in times of adversity. It can be the silver lining in a cloud-filled time of life, an anchor in a storm. We won't have immunity from troubles and trials. Doctrine and Covenants 63:34 tells us, "And the saints also shall hardly escape; nevertheless, I, the Lord, am with them, and will come down in heaven from the presence of my Father and consume the wicked with unquenchable fire."

From the time The Church of Jesus Christ of Latter-day Saints was organized, a sifting process has been evident. Those without strong testimonies are blown to and fro by the winds of criticism. Some waver when they are challenged to stand up and be counted. Only those with strong testimonies can cope with false accusations and slander. With peace in their hearts they know that the trends of the world and the criticism of men cannot alter the truths of God.

To realize that there is an ever-growing number of people in the world who have a testimony can also bring a measure of peace to our troubled world and a sense of stability to anxious times.

By having a testimony of the truthfulness of the gospel of Jesus Christ, we can know what we prefer. Indeed, we can keep our souls alive. These words Paul wrote to the Corinthians become more meaningful: "Eye hath not seen, nor ear heard, neither have entered into the heart of man, the things which God hath prepared for them that love him." (1 Corinthians 2:9.)

Our testimony can bring peace and security as we travel life's paths. What joy is ours when we can say as did Alma, "And this is not all. Do ye not suppose that I know of these things myself? Behold, I testify unto you that I do know that these things whereof I have spoken are true. And how do ye suppose that I know of their surety? Behold, I say unto you they are made known unto me by the Holy Spirit of God. Behold, I have fasted and prayed many days that I might know these things of myself. And now I do know of myself that they are true; for the Lord God hath made them manifest unto me by his Holy Spirit; and this is the spirit of revelation which is in me." (Alma 5:45-46.)

Day by day our "too small" testimonies can grow. They can furnish those needed guidelines for planning and decision making. They give us greater personal power. They provide a necessary ingredient for real spiritual progress as we follow the advice of our Savior: "But seek ye first the kingdom of God, and his righteousness; and all these things shall be added unto you." (Matthew 6:33.)

A father stood by watching his son try to move a huge boulder. The son pulled and tugged and pushed to no avail. Finally the father said, "Have you tried everything you could to move that rock?"

"Yes," said the boy as he mopped his brow. "Everything."

"No you haven't," said his father. "You haven't asked me to help you."

A wise Heavenly Father has provided opportunities for the growth of our human souls. Our testimony can fortify us against the trials we must face and can help us know we are living a part of eternity each day. Joy can be ours as we become aware of the fact that when we have done our best our Father is standing by waiting anxiously to help us if we will but ask.

Norma B. Ashton has served on the Relief Society general board and in stake and ward Relief Society and Mutual Improvement Association callings. Active in many volunteer groups, she has been a member of the governing board of Cottonwood Hospital in Salt Lake Valley and a Pink Lady at the LDS Hospital. She and her husband, Elder Marvin J. Ashton of the Council of the Twelve, have four children and thirteen grandchildren.

THE JOYS OF CHANGE

Elaine Cannon

When I had my first baby about thirty years ago, I was treated with great respect and infinite tenderness. My husband was anxious. Nurses hovered over me by the minute. My mother, who had conducted the affairs of my own arrival in her bed at home, stood by with the kind of maternal anxiety I had witnessed in her on only one other occasion. That was when I was to perform at my first piano recital before some of her friends.

I stayed in the hospital bed for ten days, scarcely lifting my arm other than to hold the new baby at feeding time. Then I moved home to mother's for further pampering. I wasn't an invalid. I was just treated like one. That's how they did things then.

We had babies nearly every year after that, whether we needed them or not. Gradually methods changed. Twelve years or so after the first baby, our last child was born. By then, having a baby was a rather simple arrangement. I was home cooking waffles for our little destroying angels almost before I could cry out for joy.

You know, there is a tender scripture in John 16:21 that reads: ". . . she remembereth no more the anguish, for joy that a [babe] is born into the world."

Travail. Change. Joy.

Is there any joy in change?

We are pregnant and then skinny. We are young and we get old. We are born and we die. We are relaxed, then the bishop comes to call. We are single, then somebody's wife (or vice versa!). Crickets sing, then suddenly it is Christmas.

Sometimes change comes swiftly, startlingly. Sometimes its pace is so gradual as to be almost unapparent. Sometimes it is announced (ready or not you shall be caught!). Sometimes change is subtle, secret, until it is too late. Often it is painful, traumatic. And sometimes it is the best thing ever to occur.

But joy?

Having a baby, holding a newborn, looking into the face of heaven is to recognize the partnership of God and change. ". . . weeping may endure for a night," said the scribe, "but joy cometh in the morning." (Psalm 30:5.)

How can we be sure?

There are two important days in a woman's life—the day she is born and the day she finds out why.

All of us have successfully accomplished the first. Now, if we can just grow in understanding of the second. That second day—the day we find out why we're born—may lengthen to a lifetime as we grow in the gospel and in understanding of the plan of life with its governing principles, until at least we see that life is change, life is learning.

There is believing. And there is knowing. There is the mighty change that must occur in the heart of each of us before we can see God, see his face, and know that he is. (See D&C 93:1.)

And then there is joy.

When we succeed in finding out why we were born, we should understand at last that we are here to be tested. Change, in all its many facets, is implicit in the test.

Change is the big challenge.

Change is pain. One of the traumas of life at any stage is change. To give up the comfortable and move away from the family hurts.

When change in our personal circumstance comes, how can we cope? What attitude will we assume if it is a negative trauma instead of a joyful moment? We can make lemonade out of the proverbial lemon. We can guard against our disposition turning sour and our inner growth being stunted by the way we react. Isn't it the matter of the lemon and the ade, after all? What a difference attitude makes in changing circumstance's impact.

We may not be able to change our circumstances, but we can change our way of responding to them.

Part of our growth and development should include getting the true perspective of life, of change and the way we filter truth. Emerson said, "This time, like all times, is a good one if you know what to do with it."

There are at least two things that will help us cope appropriately with change. One is attitude. The other is truth. We'll be better off if we can learn to look at what happens to us in a positive way—"How can I make this trauma turn into a blessing in disguise?" "Which of my Heavenly Father's principles will help me now?" We need to learn correct principles so we can govern ourselves in wisdom.

Then we must act upon truth, "That we henceforth be no more children, tossed to and fro, and carried about with every wind of doctrine, by the sleight of men, and cunning craftiness, whereby they lie in wait to deceive." (Ephesians 4:14.) We are daughters of our Heavenly Father, and counted among the people on earth today who have covenanted with God. That should make all the difference in how we respond to change.

What about change outside ourself? We live in a time of political expediency, of mass social experimentation and acceptance, of intellectual curiosity that often is too easily satisfied. But because an idea or social pattern is cleverly touted, stridently praised, or even widely practiced, we should not necessarily be assured that it is eternally valid or even sensible, nor does it mean that everyone is embracing it. It does not require our support.

Being able to make a proper value judgment about change in all its many facets and faces is critical when we have only one chance to live and this is it. Whatever we have to work with, whatever state or age we are in, we have only *now* to claim for our use. And all the rest of our life depends upon it.

As change comes that threatens our traditions, we need to know when we are conforming to the world instead of the will of God. Knowing the difference is necessary for us as daughters of God, with special missions to perform. Being able to make proper value judgments, to verify philosophical foundations, to evaluate validity of statements, perspectives, ideas—these are critically important to us all at whatever stage of life we are in.

Dr. Morowitz of Yale University has complained that schools don't teach students to examine the issues today. "As a result," said he, "we have a large cohort of young people set loose in a rapidly changing and confusing world without any conceptual tools for evaluating the extraordinary amount of information that they experience daily. Mass communication is too effective to stand without a truth filter for the recipients."

One duty of each member of The Church of Jesus Christ of Latter-day Saints is to be a "truth filter." We're in the business of training people to know truth. We'll be better at helping others if we ourselves know. People can learn this if they do not accept everything to be of equal value. Some truth matters mightily. For example, the gospel of Jesus Christ is not only true, it is important! It is critical to our salvation and exaltation. It is one of those truths that matter. That eggs go hard when they are cooked is a truth, but it just may not be as valuable a truth to acquire in one's thinking as is a sureness that the gospel is true and that Spencer W. Kimball is, in fact, God's spokesman on earth, his prophet in our day.

There are many choice and gifted people out there in the world who know many truths, but they don't know this truth. And it makes all the difference.

Intelligent consideration should be given to any form of change, any new thrust from the world, any counsel from leadership, any attitude about a trial in your life. But this requires that we do our homework, that we learn to filter truth. Finding truth should be followed by acting upon it.

The Lord has provided a system to help us make a critical analysis of change in our lives. Here are five scriptures to consider that, used together, provide a kind of formula for filtering truth:

1. "Be not conformed to this world: but be ye transformed by the renewing of your mind, that ye may prove what is that good, and acceptable, and perfect, will of God." (Romans 12:2.)

2. "For behold, the Spirit of Christ is given to every man, that he may know good from evil; wherefore, I show unto you the way to judge; for every thing which inviteth to do good, and to persuade to believe in Christ, is sent forth by the power and gift of Christ; wherefore ye may know with a perfect knowledge it is of God.

"But whatsoever thing persuadeth men to do evil, and believe not in Christ, and deny him, and serve not God, then ye may know with a perfect knowledge it is of the devil." (Moroni 7:16-17.)

3. "If any of you lack wisdom, let him ask of God, that giveth to all men liberally, and upbraideth not; and it shall be given him." (James 1:5.)

4. "But, behold, I say unto you, that you must study it out in your mind; then you must ask me if it be right, and if it is right I will cause that your bosom shall burn within you; therefore, you shall feel that it is right." (D&C 9:8.)

5. "And when ye shall receive these things, I would exhort you that ye would ask God . . . if these things are . . . true; and if ye shall ask with a sincere heart, with real intent, having faith in Christ, he will manifest the truth of it unto you, by the power of the Holy Ghost."

Elaine Cannon

(Moroni 10:4.) Truth will be made known to you by the Holy Ghost.

Let's summarize the steps:
1. Renew your mind
2. Know the system
3. Get guidance from God
4. Study it out
5. Get confirmation by the Holy Ghost

This is one way to know truth.

Wouldn't it, in fact, be well for us to remember that—

—we may not be able to change our circumstances, only our responses.

—we can learn if we do not accept every truth to be of equal value.

—all decisions and choices of any consequence whatever should be made in the perspective of gospel principles and with tender closeness to the Lord.

—there is a difference between preference and principle, and between opinion and a prophet's counsel.

President Kimball has spoken to us women plainly on this matter. He has reminded us that no matter what we read or hear, no matter what the differences of circumstances we observe in the lives of women about us, it is important for us Latter-day Saint women to understand that the Lord holds us in the highest esteem. He has entrusted to his daughters the great responsibility of bearing and nurturing children. "May you realize that in you is the control of your life and what you are going to be, what you are going to do," said President Kimball.

We can bear the babies and know that ever-wondrous joy. We can nurture the child and lovingly serve the needful, and in the process we can experience in part what the Savior did when he told the Nephites, "And now behold, my joy is full." (3 Nephi 17:20.)

Joy is a coming thing—it just isn't a now thing. We must have understood this as we voted in that large council eons ago. My understanding is that we wanted to come to earth to learn—even through suffering, for that is how learning comes. We wanted to come so much that we raised our hands and shouted, "I'll go, even if I have to live alone." "I'll go, even if I must move about crippled." "I'll go. Yes! What if my child rebels or my body withers. Let me change so I can learn, so I can live eternally."

This is how I feel, anyway.

I've lived awhile now. Having babies isn't part of my life's business anymore. Loving them still is, though, and helping them to understand what I am just beginning to value so highly: that change is joy when you deal with it according to God's eternal principles. These children grow up and leave my nest empty, but my heart full because "I have no greater joy than to hear that my children walk in truth." (3 John 1:4.)

One takes the laws irrevocably decreed and tries to match them to the trauma of change. Then the blessings come. The best blessing may well be peace. At least it seems so to me, more and more, these days. I like Shakespeare's expression about peace that is recorded in *Henry VII*, act 3, scene 2: "I feel within me a peace above all earthly dignities, a still and quiet conscience."

In that kind of change there is infinite joy.

Elaine Cannon, president of the Young Women of the Church, has been a columnist for the Deseret News *and an editor of the* Era of Youth *and the* New Era; *she is also the author of the book* Summer of My Content *and co-author of* The Mighty Change. *She and her husband, D. James Cannon, have six children and reside in Salt Lake City.*

BALANCE:
THE JOY OF
PERSPECTIVE

Anne G. Osborn

        In a recent devotional at
Brigham Young University, Bruce C. Hafen, president of
Ricks College, related the suppressed frustration of an
overworked, somewhat harassed young mother who,
when advised to "just be sure you put the Lord's work
first," blurted out in near desperation, "But what if it is
all the Lord's work?" (*Ensign*, August 1979, pp. 63-67.)
Merely perusing the titles of the chapters included in this
book reminds us of the many varied aspects in our lives
that must be balanced.

Lest we become overwhelmed by the Savior's admonition to "Be ye therefore perfect" (Matthew 5:48), let us
remember that one of the great learning experiences of
this life is not only to make the right decisions, but also
to sequence them properly. The configuration or priority
of correct choices is as important as the choices
themselves. To choose not only wisely but also timely
and well brings to us the joy of a balanced, productive
life.

There is a sense of eternalness about joy that is simply
not present in the concept of mere pleasure. I am
therefore convinced that in order to experience the joy of
a balanced life we need to sequence our priorities (and
the sometimes complex, difficult decisions they imply)
from the eternal point of view. The eternal perspective
brings our choices and challenges into sharp, clear focus.
"If we look upon life as an eternal thing . . . all happen-
ings may be put in proper perspective." (Spencer W.
Kimball, *Tragedy or Destiny?*, Deseret Book, 1977, p. 2.)

While there are surely some major decisions that
must be made between right and morally wrong choices,

43

for most of us the greater difficulty comes in choosing between two equally correct alternatives. Most choices we face are therefore not between right and wrong but between right and right. Few of us have to choose between holding family home evening and robbing a bank. More often the most difficult decisions are between equally attractive, worthy activities. Should we can the fruit that is now perfectly ripe or go on a much-needed date with our partner? Should we get in that long overdue temple session or take the children on an outing? We must have the eternal perspective to recognize that when two equally right choices are at least temporarily mutually exclusive, we should assume no burden of guilt because of our inability to do the impossible.

Almost overwhelmed by the immediate pressures of Church callings and professional responsibilities, I used to feel terribly guilty about postponing my genealogical work. Attending genealogy class in Sunday School once induced feelings of panic and near-despair as I enviously eyed the family histories and charts dating back to the 1600s that were proudly displayed by other class members. Yet I finally resolved those feelings of conflict when I realized I couldn't manage to do all righteous things simultaneously. Now that we've been asked to complete our four-generation charts by July 1981, other activities are being temporarily put aside (without guilt) while I complete that important assignment.

When we contemplate all the various aspects of our personalities that must become developed on the long pathway to perfection and exaltation, it is all too easy to despair when confronted with seemingly unreachable ideals. Somehow we Mormon women often feel we need to cook like a Julia Child or Winnifred Jardine, have the intellect and wit of an Elaine Cannon, the leadership talents of a Barbara Smith, the deep, abiding spirituality of a Camilla Kimball. And, of course, this is in addition to keeping a daily journal, becoming scriptural scholars, writing our personal history, maintaining a garden that looks like something out of the Burpee seed catalog, completing our four-generation genealogical charts, rendering compassionate service, becoming involved in community activities, fulfilling Church callings, providing a nurturing home environment for our families, and so on. For many women in the Church it may also be in addition to acquiring an education, making a living, or both.

In fact, if we weren't so often on the verge of collapse from sheer fatigue we might have the perspective to chuckle at ourselves for our sometimes unrealistic expectations and the demands we place on our own shoulders. The tasks at hand and those that lie ahead are gargantuan only if we fail to see that ordering these very activities, putting them in proper perspective, is indeed part of our mortal learning process.

The practical problems are encountered when free agency intersects the dimensions (and limitations) imposed by time. To develop and magnify our talents in the time allotted is a difficult (but "do-able") challenge. About a year and a half ago I developed a severe case of respiratory flu. After six weeks had passed I was still weak, had developed a chronic cough, and continued to feel awful. Ruefully realizing that the doctor who treats himself has a fool for a patient, I finally gave up and made an appointment with a colleague. "I can't afford to feel like this. I've got too much to do," I complained. Muttering, he punctuated his thorough physical examination with some rather pointed questions. "How many Church jobs do you hold?" "How many scientific papers did you write this last year?" "How many hours sleep do you get a night?" "How many miles a day did you say you run?" "Did you have a garden again this year and put up all your own produce?"

When he'd finally finished he put his hands on his hips, looked me sternly in the eye, and demanded, "Just exactly who or what do you think you are? Wonder

Woman? You're expecting a thirty-five-year-old woman's body to perform as it did when you were twenty-one. In fact, you're copping out. You're avoiding making decisions by trying to do *everything*. Grow up. You don't need a doctor; you need a good verbal spanking!" Sheepishly I acknowledged he was absolutely right. And I have subsequently tried to temper my choices, realizing that my strength and energy *are* limited. I still try to do too much, but at least I'm gradually getting a little better at choosing among equally worthy activities.

Elder Neal Maxwell has reminded us that the scripture "do not run faster or labor more than you have strength" (D&C 10:4) suggests "paced progress" (*Ensign*, November 1976, p. 12). I am certain that the Lord gave us that precious scripture because in his infinite wisdom he knew some of us (like me) would senselessly feel impelled to do precisely that. In the eternal realities there is simply no such thing as bionic tennis shoes or spiritual seven league boots. Wonder Woman is, after all, a comic book character.

We are so often impatient with ourselves, forgetting that the Lord himself is infinitely patient. "Continue in patience until ye are perfected" (D&C 67:13), "run with patience the race" (Hebrews 12:1), and "add to temperance patience" (2 Peter 1:6) are words of eternal worth and wisdom, were we only to heed them.

Timing is as important as content of choice. Yes, we can and *will* eventually get it all done! But that requires taking things one step at a time. It may necessitate putting some long-range goals momentarily aside as we deal with more immediate demands and the exigencies of the moment. It may require the emotional maturity to accept temporary asymmetries in the balance and rhythm of our daily lives to achieve eternal symmetry in our personal development. It is not easy, but it is possible.

In our individual and collective quest for perfection, it is not the sprinter, the saint whose spirituality is only momentarily incandescent, who wins the eternal prize. Like running a marathon, to finish, to endure to the end, is to win.

Winning itself must, of course, be viewed from the eternal perspective. All too often we yearn for the praise and prize of being first rather than the much more important process of completing the task itself. A much beloved, oft-repeated story in our family is about my mother. As a child she was a very capable, successful competitive swimmer. One day my grandfather brought several friends to watch her race in a particularly important meet. One of his friends, caught up in the enthusiasm of the competition, exclaimed, "Jeannie, if you win I'll give you fifty cents." My grandfather put his arm around her shoulders and quietly said, "Jeannie, if you *lose* and are the first one to congratulate the winner I'll give you fifty cents." Nearly fifty years later I'm sure my mother can't remember whether she won that particular race or not. But our grandfather's wisdom and proper perspective became guidelines for his future generations. Do your best, win when and if possible, but keep all things in proper perspective.

With our institutional emphasis on excellence it may become easy to envy those who we, from our limited perspective, feel have been given more or better talents, more visible callings in the Church, or more in the way of worldly goods and wealth. In a Relief Society seminar that I conducted not long ago a quiet, somewhat withdrawn sister suddenly remarked vehemently, "You know, I've been a member for over sixty years and I've *never* had an important job in the Church!" As I understand it, there is no such thing as an unimportant calling. In fact, the stewardship each currently holds is for that person the most important job in the Church. From the eternal point of view, are perhaps willingness and diligence not equally important with worthiness? We all have been given at least one gift that, if utilized to the fullest, will bring other opportunities for growth and service. Like Alma, we should learn to be content with those things allotted to us (see Alma 29:3), realizing that we also have the open invitation to "seek earnestly the best gifts" (D&C 46:8).

To me, the parable of the talents teaches us a startlingly important but subtle point: those who truly magnify their talents, regardless of their type or number, receive the identical eternal reward. When the talents were originally distributed, the individual who was given only two (that is, he received neither the least nor the most) might well have complained either that he didn't receive more or that he didn't particularly like the ones he got. Yet he diligently, faithfully worked to utilize and increase his own assigned stewardship. There is an unusual feature about celestial arithmetic: when the final accounting came due the servant who had faithfully doubled his two talents, thereby having four, received the same accolade from the Lord as did the one who had originally been given five and ended up with ten. Like the latecomer to the vineyard who labored only an hour yet nevertheless completed his assigned task, each of us will receive whatsoever reward is right. A comforting concept for us converts!

It is trite but nevertheless true that each of us is unique. Like a multifaceted diamond, we are polished one surface at a time. Like that precious jewel, no two of us are alike. The Lord certainly never intended us to render the same service or follow identical schedules of personal development. There is an eternal balance not only between people, but in the very rhythm of each individual's life itself. My children will probably never appear in the ward Christmas program wearing stunning outfits I carefully crafted for them. I've learned to sew people but not clothes! While I can and do admire the talent of those who have, I won't feel guilty about clothing family in "store-bought" dresses.

From the eternal point of view it is also important to distinguish between the things of God and the things of man. As an example, formal educational degrees—things of man—are relatively unimportant from the eternal point of view. The personal qualities that the educational process enhances are not. In the eternities no one will likely remember—or even care—about the presence or absence of letters following our names. Perhaps the only honorifics that will truly matter are those like Brother, Sister, Elder, Mother, Father. While the earthly medical degree I worked so long and hard to attain has permitted me to render a very special type of service, perhaps even more important are the qualities of compassion, intellectual discipline, decision-making, analytical skills, and faith that were honed and enriched by that rigorous professional training. These are portable, eternal qualities that can and will rise with us in the resurrection. Compassion is always employable. Unlike technological skills, faith and intellectual discipline do not become obsolete.

The temporary asymmetries in life induced by circumstance will, if we can but remain faithful, become balanced in the eternities. Since I am unmarried at age thirty-six, it is easy for me to envy wistfully the young mother who lovingly cradles her child in her arms (forgetting the many dirty diapers and sleepless nights she's endured). Conversely, it is easy for the young mother with four children under the age of six to envy the seemingly carefree, glamorous life of a career woman (forgetting the long years of dedicated study and personal sacrifice that were prerequisites).

The upwardly mobile career woman may have to struggle to render compassionate service. The busy housewife or young mother, pressed to the wall by the immediate needs of her family, may have to struggle to study the scriptures and grow intellectually. The widow struggling with loneliness may have to make a determined effort to brighten the lives of those around her.

There are celestial compensations and earthly challenges in every circumstance. With some forethought, it is possible to fulfill partially some of each other's needs. I sometimes become a "mother for an evening," baby-sitting so I enjoy her children while their mother relishes a rare moment of peaceful freedom!

Finally, let us remember that it is quite literally the small and simple things out of which great things are brought to pass. The small and seemingly insignificant choices we continually make can become either stumbling blocks or stepping-stones on the pathway to a joyful, balanced day-to-day life and—ultimately—eternal life and exaltation.

Let us also be realistic, not expecting or demanding more of ourselves than the Lord does. Exaltation is not an instant process. Life is not leaping tall buildings at a single bound. It is more like carefully pacing ourselves, marshaling our precious energy and spiritual resources so that we *can* mount those steps one at a time. And perhaps we may even develop the eternal sense to pause a moment for rest, reflection, and contemplation of how far we've actually come. Then, as we resolutely turn our hearts and faces upwards, we rejoice in the wonders and delights that surely lie ahead.

Of this I am certain: the gospel with its eternal perspective adds a much-needed dimension of joy that I had never believed possible. New horizons, entire new vistas are opened only by the gospel of Jesus Christ. Life has balance, meaning, and a firm foundation that make personal possibilities truly infinite.

A convert to the Church, Anne Osborn teaches New Testament and Book of Mormon classes at the Institute of Religion, University of Utah. By profession she is a physician and associate professor of radiology at the University of Utah College of Medicine. She is a member of the Relief Society general board and a former member of the Sunday School board.

THE JOYS OF MOTHERHOOD

Petrea Kelly

Lofty, beautiful, and serene, a celestial orb glistens in a luminescent sky. Far below on the frontier of a dark wilderness in a tiny fortress live some strangers from the splendid place above. Their home is an outpost, reflecting some of the glory of the celestial homeland but surrounded by darkness and constantly under attack.

Now as day dawns a woman in the outpost arises from sleep and on her knees opens the communication lines between her home and the orb above. A conduit sheds light and strength upon her, and serenity fills her heart, peace floods her soul, and light overflows from within her. The wilderness pulls away from her bastion, overwhelmed by the light. She turns to her sacred books from the holy home above, seeking guidance from this glorious source of light.

A baby cries; she closes the books and turns away. Children's voices intrude on her thoughts. Diapers, breakfast, lost socks to find, lunches to prepare. "I'm late, honey; hurry and gather the children for family prayer." "Why is that boy always late? He's keeping the whole family waiting." "Brent had his eyes open during the prayer." "How do you know? You peeked." The conduit of light from above begins to fade. The wilderness moves closer to the little outpost; black tendrils slither around the doors, seeking a tiny opening, testing, probing.

Stacks of dishes, mountains of laundry, baskets of mending, jars and cans and boxes and pots of food. Machines humming, stove cooking, children playing, baby crying, television speaking—loud, authoritarian, educated voices: "Women who stay at home and are only housewives are robbing themselves and society of the contributions they could make. Housework is mindless work. To be a housewife is a fate worse than death. Children would be better raised by experts in child care centers rather than left to amateur mothers." Black tendrils wrap around and around the TV antenna.

The children become bored; the woman draws them around her and teaches them, reads stories, gives hugs and kisses. Later when the children are napping, she has time for some reading. "Parents have no right to impose their ideas on children. Never say 'no' to your children. Never criticize, always praise. Never spank. Never punish. If the child is not successful, it is the parents who have failed."

"Oh, Johnny, are you writing on the walls again?"

The father and children come back to the outpost from their excursions into the wilderness. Some of them still have darkness clinging to them. "But everyone else gets to." "I'm too dumb to do this math." "Sorry I can't do my chores—I've got tons of homework, and besides it's Mutual." The woman works to dispel the darkness and help her family return to the light. A friend calls: "I'm discouraged and you make me feel guilty. I don't see why you try so hard when it's not worth it. What do you expect, perfection?"

With evening comes more darkness. "Hurry, hurry, no time to talk." "So much to do, not enough time." "More money, we need more things." The woman goes about searching out shadows and tendrils; pushing them out, locking the doors and windows against them. She makes room for light, strengthens her defenses, and stockpiles ammunition for another day of battle. "Let's read a story from the Bible." "Tell me what you did today that made you happy." "What do you think you can do tomorrow that will help you and Johnny get along better?" "Time for family prayer." "Could I listen to your prayers?" "I'll tuck you in bed when you're ready." "Of course, I have time to listen to you."

In the dark of the night the woman and her husband look out and note with satisfaction that the wilderness is a fraction of an inch farther away than yesterday. They kneel again and catch a tiny glimmer of the splendor they have part in creating, and they are dazzled by the glory.

Science fiction? Not at all, for scattered about upon the earth are small outposts of the kingdom of God where men and women join with God in creation. Not just the creation that ends with the birth of a child, but the ongoing creation of celestial homes that begins at the altar and continues throughout eternity.

In creating a home and making it function we have much more freedom and responsibility than do people in any other occupation in the world. They are always restricted by bosses and supervisors, stockholders, the buying public, or the realities of the marketplace—in other words, they are tied to the earth. Homemakers, on the other hand, can soar to heaven, for theirs is a heavenly and celestial business. The homes we create in partnership with our husbands and the Lord are training grounds for the celestial kingdom.

Joseph Smith stated that the gospel was restored to prepare a people for the millennial reign of Christ. It is our goal to be the people he was talking about; however, we do not become a people fit to live with the Savior in only the three or four hours a week that we spend in church. Surely this must be the reason our leaders put so much emphasis on the home and family, for it is in our homes that we learn to live with the Savior. Here we learn to live the law we will live forever, and if we are willing to have a telestial home with disorder, bickering, selfishness, and irreverence, that is the law we will learn to live and we will certainly not be prepared to live a higher order.

A celestial home is difficult to achieve in this world, particularly at this time. It requires that we know what we are aiming for and then that we toil endlessly toward that target—even on the days when the children are ill, the toilet floods over, the washing machine breaks down, someone misses the school bus, and the husband comes home after a bad day at his work and notices gum embedded in the carpet. Even on days like this we must keep our sights on heaven and remind ourselves constantly that our goal is a celestial home, and though all the powers of confusion and darkness gather against us, they shall not prevail. Surely the harder we try and the closer we come to our goal, the greater will be the forces from outside that will try to defeat us, for Satan has great power and can rally tremendous forces to thwart the works of God. But we also have greater power in our partner, the Lord. With our own best efforts and the blessings of the Lord we cannot fail.

There are times when none of us can remember the right things to do, when we are mired in everyday life and despair. It is in anticipation of these times that we must write out our goals and desires. It is good to start with a broad statement like "We want to establish a heavenly home so all the members of our family can learn to live with Christ." But this is only a beginning. Then we must break this large goal down into smaller and smaller chunks until our dreams and our daily lives are in harmony.

Viewed from this eternal perspective, priorities begin to fall into place, and we realize that family and individual prayers are the most important things we do all day, that family scripture study is of more value than breakfast, and that it is more important to teach our children to obey the commandments than it is to teach them to brush their teeth. We view family home evening as a welcome and valuable tool rather than an obligation. We amplify the lessons taught in Sunday School and Primary and Young Women and help our children apply them in their lives. Every experience, almost every breath, becomes a part of the celestial fabric of our home.

As we attempt to maintain holy homes, we come to

realize that we must start with ourselves—our own minds, bodies, and spirits must be in top form. Once again the day-to-day activities fall into place. Proper diet, exercise, prayer, scripture study, and talent development all fall into place before such worldly demands as soap operas, idle gossip, window shopping, and sometimes even clubs, community service, and PTA. <u>Once we are sure of our goals and have confirmed them with the Lord, it becomes easier to sort out the demands of the world and know which to accept, which to reject, and which to postpone.</u> If we are in tune with the Lord, he will inspire us and help us to be creative in solving problems and help us avoid possible dangers even before we are aware of them.

Celestial homes may be large or small, rich or poor. The families may range from a couple to a dozen or more. The home might be serene or bustling. The possible varieties are endless, but all celestial homes do share some qualities—the same ones that the Lord prescribes for the temples, which are his other homes on earth.

"Organize yourselves; prepare every needful thing; and establish a house, even a house of <u>prayer,</u> a house of <u>fasting,</u> a house of <u>faith,</u> a house of <u>learning,</u> a house of <u>glory,</u> a house of <u>order,</u> <u>a house of God</u>." (D&C 88:119.)

This is the yardstick against which we can measure our individual homes. If they do not measure up, they are not outposts of the kingdom of God, and we can see at once where we must improve.

Because my own children are still young, I feel that I am a bit of an apprentice mother with a great deal to learn. I cannot speak about motherhood from the lofty heights of experience. But from the heat of the battle perhaps I can send out a few bulletins. My husband and I recently completed a project which to us serves as a kind of analogy for celestial family building—we built a house.

From the time when both of us were young and we didn't even know each other, we had dream houses in mind. Mine was full of loved ones, sunshine, warmth, creativity, smells of good things cooking, and surrounded by trees and flowers. His was a peaceful haven from the world, warm and cozy with a fire in the fireplace, a bookcase full of books, his favorite music playing, and the smell of good things cooking. When we met and married, the building of that house came high on our list of priorities. The scriptures taught us that we would someday have the opportunity to create worlds if we prepared for that responsibility in this life. We felt that creating our physical environment here on the earth would be a wise use of our stewardship and good training. We believed in Winston Churchill's statement: "First we shape our buildings; thereafter they shape us." We spent years studying homes by the master designers and architects, looking at homes, dreaming and praying. Finally we found the ideal location for the house—and then our planning began in earnest. As we paid for the property we drew house plans, collected ideas from books, magazines, and other homes, studied the ideal homes, and prayed some more. We kept our ideas in a folder, then a box, then several boxes.

We tried to draw our own house plans, but our drawings never quite matched the ideal in our minds, so we searched for a designer to help us. We visited homes built by several architects until finally, after much searching, we found one who shared our ideas of what a home should be and was willing to help us plan the kind of home we wanted. In fact, he added dimensions we could not have conceived of because of his own special abilities. Throughout the planning and building we prayed for help and guidance, and our prayers were answered often in surprising ways.

Builders told us we could not build the home we had in mind for the money we could afford to spend. Some told us to throw away our dreams and settle for something more ordinary. "A box is the easiest thing to build and the cheapest way to go," they said. But we were not interested in the easiest thing to do; we had a dream. So we decided to build it ourselves. The time of building was exciting—and discouraging. It seemed to take forever, but finally there would be a footing, a foundation, a wall. One small step at a time, the house took shape. Sometimes we made mistakes and had to do something over. Other times we had to compromise and settle for less than the ideal. Often we went back to the designer and the blueprints for clarification and help. We worked very hard day after day, sometimes doing big impressive things like putting up a wall or nailing down a floor; but more often doing chores that didn't show but were still important. We also did extra things that no contractor would have bothered with, like laying extra layers of insulation around the bathtubs. (We once lived in a house where we were sure the bathtub had been placed directly on the permafrost.)

We did much of the work ourselves, but occasionally it was necessary to hire experts who possessed skills or tools we did not have. Usually this was a satisfactory arrangement, but other times we found that with a little trial and error, we could learn the new skill, buy a few tools, and do a better job because we cared and had a total vision of the place, while the expert would see only a specific job to be done as quickly as possible.

At last the big day arrived. We packed up our belongings for the tenth time in as many years and moved into our dream home. It is not quite perfect, but it is warm, full of people we love, sunshine, creativity, books, music, and the smells of good things cooking—and sometimes it is even peaceful and quiet after midnight and before 6 A.M.

Building a celestial family is in many ways a parallel experience. First we have the dream independent of reality. We may not quite reach it in this life, but it is useful to keep in the backs of our minds. Getting married is like finding the perfect spot for the house. We now know exactly what we have to work with and what the challenges will be. This is the time when we choose the designer. There are many in the world who would tell us how to build our family and rear our children; but we must be careful of their advice, for their viewpoint is limited to this world and is sometimes warped and frequently changes as new philosophies become the vogue. The only designer with the eternal perspective is the Lord. His blueprint is contained in the scriptures and can be confirmed in us constantly through personal revelation. If we seek out his blueprint and study and follow it, he will add new dimensions we could not have conceived of on our own.

The work of building families, like that of building houses, is often frustrating and mundane. The results are sometimes slow in coming, but occasionally there is a bright moment when we seem to be making progress and we are encouraged to keep on. We make mistakes and sometimes have to compromise, but if we maintain contact with our designer and study the blueprint, we can correct mistakes and solve the problems. Because we are building our dream family, we can do the little extras that no experts would consider worth the labor. We can do more than keep our children fed and dressed—we can stimulate their bodies and minds and spirits so that they can achieve their divine potential.

Occasionally it is necessary to hire experts to help us with our families: doctors, dentists, schoolteachers, music and dance teachers, coaches, child care experts, and so forth. We must be careful not to get too many experts involved in doing our job or we may turn our responsibilities over to people who have not seen the blueprint we are following. Sometimes it is even necessary to violate the advice of the so-called experts just as we had to ignore the builders who told us we couldn't build the kind of house we had in mind. We must stick by our blueprint even if it isn't the fashionable way to run a family or is different from every other family in the neighborhood.

As we found in building the house, sometimes we can become expert in certain areas and create better results than even the experts. I feel this is particularly true in the overabundance of teachers we sometimes turn our children over to, from preschool through music, art, drama, sewing, cooking, 4-H, Scouting, baseball, football, soccer, and so on. If we are not careful, before we know it our children are being taught a great deal in little compartments, but they spend so little time at home that we never get around to teaching them the total picture. We must also work closely with the experts we choose to help us rear our children, just as a builder works with each subcontractor to make sure he follows the blueprint and the finished product has unity and fulfills its original purpose.

Unlike a house, a family is never finished. We move to different stages in the construction as our children grow up and their needs become different. The blueprint and foundation established in the very early years are valid throughout our lives. The marvelous thing about our scriptural blueprint is that it contains the plan for whatever stage we might be in at the moment.

There is great satisfaction in building a house, but that is nothing compared to the overwhelming joy in building an outpost of the kingdom of God. The role of mothers and fathers is sometimes downplayed in our society, but I think that those who scorn our work might not have tasted the joy that comes from understanding the glory of what we are doing. It seems to me that two things are necessary to joyful motherhood. I call them preparation and excellence.

Before a house can be built, a great deal of preparation must be made. Builders must learn certain skills. Plans must be prepared based on knowledge of the building site, the type of home desired, the building materials available, the climate, and the desires of the eventual inhabitants. A mother (and a father too) must prepare in order to be successful. We all built cabins or tree houses as children, planning as we built, scavenging what materials we could find. The ones I remember building always leaned a little, were rather drafty, and tended to fall down in the smallest breeze. We certainly can't have a heavenly home if we build like that!

Mothers-to-be would be wise to learn every possible homemaking, budgeting, interior decorating, and child-care skill they possibly can. As mothers we need to continue to learn these things and improve our abilities as we go along. The woman who fails to learn these things before marriage will have to do some heavy on-the-job cramming in order to run a successful home. Remember the Lord's pattern for his house in section 88 of the Doctrine and Covenants—one of the keys is a house of order. Homemaking skills can ensure that we do have an orderly house.

When one builds a house, not all the preparation is done on the site. At the same time the plans are being drawn, many other things are being prepared that will be part of the eventual house. Trees are being cut and made into lumber; wire is being made along with plumbing tape, tile, linoleum, glass, and nails. All these things and many more will come together to make the house. In section 88 the Lord does not say that it is enough to just have an orderly house; he also commands us to prepare ourselves to have houses of learning, houses of faith, houses of prayer, and houses of fasting.

This kind of preparation is a lifelong pursuit. We set the tone in our homes. We are like springs from which our families drink; we must be full and generous or they will perish. Our preparation must give us a reservoir of learning and faith. We refill our reservoir through prayer and fasting and in many other ways unique to each individual. Some women have a few years between high school and marriage in which to prepare. We can go to school, work, travel, deal with people in many situations, go on missions, develop our talents, and broaden our interests. One of the saddest things I see is young women in those in-between years who are just waiting to get married—nothing else—just waiting. Mothers with four children under five would give anything for the time those single women have to fill their reservoirs! If a young woman has a few years to herself, she should spend them very carefully making sure that she is filling her reservoir to the brim. Of course, the woman who marries young still has the obligation to prepare and refill her reservoir as she goes along, and the woman who marries late cannot rest on her laurels and think she did all the necessary preparation before marriage.

Once in college I heard someone talk about the importance of having both a vocation and an avocation—a trade and a love. For women homemaking must be at least our vocation (for some, it might be an avocation as well). We might also prepare for another vocation, but in addition we should cultivate as many avocations as we would like. Women who have an avocation of music seem to be particularly blessed, and their families are too. I have seen women enrich their families with their abilities in art, science, mathematics, gardening, sewing, cooking, interior decorating, carpentry, sports, shopping, nursing—there are as many possibilities as there are women. My own avocations include literature and the study of history. One of the things I really enjoyed doing in college was writing research papers, and this training has served me in good stead. Our children love to learn new things, and I think one of the reasons for this is that from their earliest days we have looked up the answers to their questions together. When we are all hauling out encyclopedias and reference books to explore the depth of the Atlantic Ocean, the names of all the planets in the universe, or the life of Mozart, I feel that ours is truly a house of learning. Besides blessing our families, our avocations feed the hidden springs in our reservoirs. I find that a few minutes of reading poetry or a good short story will lift my spirits on the most dismal days, and if I say my prayers often and have a good history book to read while nursing the baby, I'm practically immune to frustration.

All this worldly learning is of no value to our families if we neglect the spiritual preparation. The Lord described a house of faith, prayer, and fasting as well as order and learning. We need to cultivate our testimonies as well as our talents, and to study the scriptures as well as our textbooks. The most beautiful description of a prepared woman that I know of is in Proverbs 31:10-31. The poet uses physical examples, but many of the images serve on more than one level. The entire passage is worthy of our attention, but here are just a few examples:

"She is like the merchants' ships; she bringeth her food from afar." Not just food, I think, but a whole cargo of physical, emotional, and spiritual refreshment for her family.

"She girdeth her loins with strength, and strengtheneth her arms." She's on a jogging program, no doubt, which makes her strong and healthy and improves her mental outlook; but she also has a spiritual exercise program of scripture study, prayer, and fasting designed to keep her faith strong.

"Her candle goeth not out by night." Is she merely making Raggedy Ann dolls for Christmas? No, I think her testimony is a shining light to her family even in the darkest times.

"She openeth her mouth with wisdom; and in her tongue is the law of kindness." That attribute must be thoughtfully considered.

There are houses and then there are HOUSES. The worst examples of houses (lowercase) I can think of were built by the military during World War II—whole towns of them. Obviously designed and built by men who cared nothing about the families who would eventually live in them, the houses were built out of the cheapest materials available, with inconvenient floor plans and disaster area kitchens. HOUSES (uppercase), on the other hand, are built and planned with love and care. They don't have to be expensive, but the best materials available are used in them, and they are all well planned for the needs of the family who will live there.

That is the difference between just an ordinary job of mothering and approaching our duties with an attitude of excellence. The Lord is not interested in living in a spiritual box even if it is the easiest and cheapest. All one has to do is look at a sunset, a starry night, or a butterfly's wing to realize he is not interested in cheap and easy. He wants a house of glory, a house of God.

Christ promised us a more abundant life if we would follow his teachings. He taught that going the second mile in any task brings joy and abundance. If we just do the minimum requirements as mothers, it is easy to be frustrated and feel that our job is demeaning. If we rise above the minimum and work to make motherhood a work of art, we will experience joy. Take, for example, the rather onerous task of changing diapers. It is a necessity and we can treat it as an evil and be very unhappy about doing it over and over again. Or we can see it as a part of nurturing a precious human being, in which case we change the diaper as soon as it is necessary, making sure the child is comfortable and happy and clean and that the dry diaper fits well. We take care of the soiled diaper at once (they do not improve with age). We can even use this time alone with our baby to give him some special love and attention; this is a good time to teach him to find his nose, hair, and eyes. When we approach the job this way, we even get a certain amount of satisfaction out of it, and why not? We have to do it anyway. It's a matter of choice—do we want to build military housing or a house of glory?

Excellence in living the gospel is what separates our little outposts from the rest of the world. We must try harder to be more in tune with the Lord, to know our blueprints (the scriptures) better, to teach our children better, to prepare more beautiful and nutritious meals, to acquire all the homemaking skills, to develop our talents. There is nothing wrong with being that much-maligned creature, the "Mormon Supermother," for it is within all of us to do it. Not that we all have to be alike, however. One supermother might teach her children to sing, another might be able to help them learn math, and another might take them skiing. The whats and hows are not important, but the attitude is. If we are constantly trying to improve and rise above the earth, we are following "a more excellent way." It is difficult for me to write this because my own performance often falls short of my ideals, but I'm struggling along day by day trying to break bad and sloppy habits and occasionally seeing a little light in the distance that gives me the courage to keep trying.

One of my husband's and my most challenging tasks over the years has been to instill this desire for excellence in our children. We wanted them to learn some social graces so they could be comfortable as they grew up and found themselves in various social situations. We've spent some pretty dreadful times in restaurants with them, but by the time they are seven or eight we are no longer embarrassed to be seen with them. We've also regularly had fancy meals at home with the Sunday-best dishes and company manners; they now look forward to a fondue or an experimental meal of foods from another country.

Little things mean a lot in the pursuit of excellence. My husband feels that plastic drinking glasses are an affront to his teeth. We suffer through a lot of breakage to maintain our standard of glass drinking glasses, but we hope our children are developing a respect for excellence and high standards at the same time.

Summers used to be a frustrating time when we never quite seemed to be able to get together; in fact, we felt that our summers were tearing our family apart. That certainly didn't fit the blueprint we had for our family, so we took some direct and positive action and developed a complete summer program tailored to the Kelly family. There have been at least two benefits from this action: first, the family is closer and more loving, and second, we have a ready-made vehicle to teach our children the gospel and our philosophy. We have a little "school" every morning in the summer. My husband and I plan the curriculum to instill the values we consider important in our children. I often do the same sort of thing with the preschoolers during the winter. This gives me a chance to reinforce family home evening lessons and teach righteous behavior on a daily basis.

Our children are aware, to some extent, of our goals and family hopes because we talk about them often. In addition, I often post little sayings or scriptures around the house where I think they will be noticed. One couple we know has a brilliant way of keeping their dreams and aspirations before their children at all times. Kieth and Dagny Merrill had special tiles made when they built their home. These tiles are laid in the kitchen counter where the children often eat. Each tile contains a special thought, such as "I am a child of God," "We will make our home like heaven," "I am important because I belong to this family who loves me," and "Happiness does not depend on what happens to the outside of you, but what happens on the inside of you." Surely living with such thoughts day after day allows their children to absorb the philosophy the parents are trying to teach.

Excellence is rewarding in so many ways. We love our tasks, we grow in doing them, our families excel, and heaven smiles on our efforts. Most of all, happiness and love and the glory of God fill our homes, and they truly are houses of order, faith, prayer, fasting, learning, and glory. Excellence does not imply a long face and only a shoulder-to-the-wheel attitude. Family life is just too much fun to spend all our time being serious. A sense of humor is one of the most valuable tools to achieve excellence. Without it we can become too critical, and it is easy to become discouraged when we make mistakes and backslide a little. Our humor should never be at the expense of others or be unkind, but it is healthy to be able to laugh at our own mistakes, pick up the pieces, and start over. In fact, I think humor and excellence go together. The other evening when I dropped some ice cubes on the floor, everything stopped and the whole family seemed to hold its breath for a moment until I laughed about it and made a little joke. There seemed to be a collective sigh of relief, and the atmosphere of love and peace returned. Had my reaction been different, I would have destroyed the heavenly spirit for the whole evening for all ten of us.

As mothers, our work is not washing diapers and mending holes in jeans—that is what we spend much of our time doing, but it is not our work. Our work is rearing children, but it is much more than that, for we rear our children to be successful, to fulfill their potential. We might dream of their becoming president or a star of stage and screen or even a General Authority, but even in such dreams we are being shortsighted. For them to be successful, to reach their potential, they must inherit the celestial kingdom. The little people with whom we share our homes are more than gifts from God. They are gods in embryo themselves. Our work is to help them realize that awe-inspiring fact and then to live so that they will not fall short of their divine potential.

Jeans may have to be mended and dishes washed, gardens tended, floors swept, and beds made, but all these things are gifts of God to us. They are tools that we may use to develop our own divinity and help our children develop theirs. We don't become righteous in spite of dishes, diapers, and dirty floors, but through them. We sweep floors, weed gardens, tend babies, and learn and grow—our spirits along with our bodies. No one grows in a vacuum. One does not just sit in a white room and think great thoughts and thus become divine. The earth and everything on it are designed to function as a great schoolroom; everything we need to develop our celestiality is here. Divinity is developed in us as we use the tools of the earth to create our own celestial environments—houses of God. Thus clean floors, made beds, and neat cupboards are part of this celestial environment, and we must teach our children this, starting with making their own bed at age three or picking up a toy at age two.

Our celestial environments are more than orderly and clean, they are also places of learning. This might imply family scripture study, places of faith and prayer and fasting. Here we see how family prayer, teaching our children to pray, family home evenings, and attending church together help to create a celestial environment. Then if we also make our home a house of glory where love abounds and our every action and word are a form of worship of God, then we have left behind the trappings of a telestial world, and our little outposts can take their places among the stars.

Motherhood *is* joyful. It is exciting, challenging, and fun; it demands all our best efforts. Motherhood is creation of children and of the homes to nurture them in. Motherhood is partnership with husbands and the Lord. May we all catch a glimmer of the splendor we can create in our own outposts of the kingdom of God.

Petrea Kelly, who has eight children, is mother education teacher in the Highland Utah First Ward. She filled a mission to the North British Mission and has a bachelor's degree in English and education from Brigham Young University. She is married to Brian K. Kelly, managing editor of the New Era.

FAMILY JOYS

Doralee Durham Madsen

It was 5:30 in the afternoon of a very ordinary day. I had just finished teaching my last piano student of the afternoon when Richie came to me to remind me that he had to be at Skyline High School at 6:10 for make-up call for the play he was in. Kristin had only fifteen minutes to get to her music lesson (a ten-minute drive away), and Melissa was busy in the kitchen browning ten pounds of hamburger for the seminary party. Michael couldn't find his soccer shorts, and game time was at 6:15 sharp. Wallace had discovered his sisters' nail polish, and Asheley, our new baby, needed to be nursed. Richard, my husband, would be home in thirty minutes for his quick bite to eat prior to his church meeting, and couldn't I possibly drop Suzanne and Annette off at the library so they could pick up the needed reference books for their school reports? And I must not forget to pick up DeDee and Allyson from the birthday party.

Confusing, some may say. Unreal, others may declare. Frustrating, many exclaim. Joyful, I would add.

Our home buzzes with a variety of personalities and is sparked by many interests. At times, life does get very confusing, hectic, and frustrating. At these recurring moments I try to recall the words of Lehi to his son Jacob, spoken over two thousand years ago, but so applicable today. "For it must needs be, that there is an opposition in all things. If not so, . . . righteousness could not be brought to pass, neither wickedness, neither holiness nor misery, neither good nor bad." (2 Nephi 2:11.)

So as we try to meet the needs of each individual in our family and to give each the opportunity to grow by exploring this fascinating world, often the efforts turn into anger, disappointment, and confusion. But if the confusion didn't reign at times, then we would not relish the joy so gratefully.

To some individuals family living can be very trying. But we can capitalize on the joy of family life when we understand that we are living the Lord's plan. The Lord meant for us to learn to share, to fail, to succeed, to laugh and cry together, experience sorrow and happiness, for he created the family unit where this all takes place. After Adam's creation and placement in the Garden of Eden he was told to "dress and keep" the garden. Our scriptures further tell us that God told Adam he was not to live alone. (Genesis 2:18.) A family unit was created that was soon challenged by opposition. Enlightenment appears from 2 Nephi 2:25 when we learn that "Adam fell that men might be; and men are, that they might have joy." Notice the plural use of the word *men*. We could insert in the scripture the word *family*, also plural: "*families* might be; and *families* are, that they might have joy."

How can we experience this joy that was meant to be? It will not be found in the acquisition of material things or possessions, and it may not come with numbers of immediate family members, or the place we live, or the schools we attend, or the jobs we have. The joy we experience must come from within. It must come from within each individual. As Richard Wagner put it, "Joy is not in things, it is in us."

After four decades of living on this earth and first-hand experience in at least three family groups—the family I was born into, the family my husband and I have brought into the world, and the family I have married into—I have concluded that the real joy of family life, the kind of joy that comes from within, is realized through (1) recognition of the family unit as eternal; (2) support of each other, which involves service to one another and doing things together; and (3) living the law of obedience.

These three are bound by our continual love for one another. The Prophet Joseph Smith taught us that when the Savior appears again we shall see him as "a man like ourselves. And that same sociality which exists among us here will exist among us there, only it will be coupled with eternal glory, which glory we do not now enjoy." (D&C 130:1-2.) Isn't it a wonderful doctrine to realize that we will live in our same family units, eternally, and enjoy even greater happiness? This can give us the incentive to strive for inner joy within the family.

Did you ever ponder the question of which came first, the chicken or the egg? We might ponder a similar question: when does a family unit begin? Does it begin when one first becomes conscious of belonging to a family as a young child? Does it begin when parents bring their first sweet spirit into the world as a baby? Does the vision of the eternal family unit unfold as grandparents look over their posterity of grandchildren and great-grandchildren? This is a circular question, for the family as the basic unit of society in our church is eternal. As family members become aware of their family circle, their joy is enriched.

As I was driving home from town one day, one of my small children who was in the car with me pointed to a local pizza restaurant and exclaimed, "There's where Grandpa likes to go!" Now, Grandpa doesn't usually make a habit of eating there, but a few summers ago he had me buy pizza at that particular restaurant for the children's lunch break when we were helping him clean out his old family home following the death of his mother. To the teenagers helping their grandfather, this was a rich, bonding experience. As we looked in old trunks together, walked over the sleeping porch where five active boys of another generation had bunked, listened to family stories sparked by precious memorabilia, and carted boxes of personal goods to the car, we all felt a closeness to our grandparents and great-grandparents. The younger children sensed that Saturday activity as an adventure with their grandfather. As they rolled the ball down their great-grandmother's long, grassy yard for one last time, and raced to see who could catch it first, we all felt a closeness and thankfulness for our extended family unit.

Grandpa had made the necessary chore of cleaning out this family home interesting, educational, and memorable, as well as fun for all with the special treat of pizza for lunch, which the children still relate to this incident.

As a budding author of twelve, I realized a degree of joy when a devoted grandfather took the time and interest in his grandchild to put together my many poems that had been written and created over a summer's time. These poems came back to me in the form of a little "published" book as a birthday present one year. To this day this little booklet is a personal treasure to me and a great example of a grandparent's love.

Another kind of happiness is experienced each summer when we pile twelve bodies of varying sizes into one car along with necessary baggage and food and proceed the seven hundred or so miles from our home to the California beaches each summer. We never stop for anything except gas, accept the stares of passing motorists, and experience complete exhaustion coupled with delight upon arriving safely at our destination. We are always welcome at the lovely condominium of our children's paternal grandparents. They live in our city also, but travel to California as often as possible for the benefits of the lower altitudes.

Our family experienced a beautiful delight one summer when the maternal grandparents, also of our city, shared their vacation with us, jumping in the ocean waves with the children, sightseeing along the coastal towns together, sharing the excitement of Sea World, and experiencing the fun of discovering new eating establishments. This delight was further extended when the other grandparents, the owners of the condominium, dropped in on us unexpectedly for an added bonus to our trip. It didn't matter that there were so many in the two-bedroom condominium. We rolled out more sleeping bags, ate in shifts, and had a perfectly delightful time sharing this new experience with four grandparents.

It is special to gather at Christmas with cousins, grandparents, aunts, and uncles, and, along with the old familiar carols, sing the beautiful songs composed by my father's father for this special season. Though he has passed away, his memory lingers on through his music. Grandpa's songs are a tradition of Christmas. Singing them with loved ones is "Joy to the World"!

Our mountain home is the result of great love through the generations for one another. This favorite family spot, nestled in the trees of Big Cottonwood Canyon, came to pass because of a father's love for his native land of Norway. Wanting this love to continue, he willed the land to his children, who have shared it with their children and their children. As four generations experienced this beautiful scenery and happy days away from the routines of city life, a small glimpse of the eternal family unit passes by.

Joy comes to the family who serve each other, who support each other, and who do things together, even if not always convenient for everyone. Our children have had good secretarial training as they have helped their father by scheduling many church appointments and interviews. It's not always easy to call someone you don't know to set up an appointment for a prearranged time. As they have worked side by side with him in his business, they have received a better understanding of his work, as well as having a special private time with him. As early as age three or four they begin taking their turns "helping" Dad out at work. As they get older they are able to earn a little money by dusting, vacuuming, and cleaning the restrooms at his business. The children are learning the value of the dollar, the importance of hard, honest work, the expertise of cleanliness, and the fun of helping and being with their dad. Joy? I'll never forget the time four of us had to sacrifice something we wanted to do because Dad needed someone at his business after closing hours to supervise a repair project. Dad could not be there because he had obligations at a church meeting. I suppose that only one of us needed to hurry to the business that night (without dinner), but three others came so that the one wouldn't have to wait alone. Joy is support!

For six weeks each summer we do not gather as a family for an evening meal. Many times at ten o'clock at night one of the children will ask, "Did we have any dinner tonight?" About the age of nine our girls began playing in a girls' softball program, and as the boys have now come along, a typical summer evening has found at least three games being played in one evening that we would like to support. More than once we have eaten grapes, cheese, and juice for dinner on the lawn of one of the local softball fields while cheering for one of the children, then rushed to another diamond to see the end of another game. One year we ran to softball, baseball, and soccer games all in one evening! The little ones love to go to the games and provide a cheering section, complete with pom-poms. Those who have now graduated from this Little League activity give great support as they continue to go and support their younger brothers and sisters. The youngest child can hardly wait until it is his turn to play!

The athletic programs in the school system provide excellent opportunities for young people's development and growth. It is exciting to see the development of the game techniques from grade school level to senior high school levels. We love to go as a family to support the various teams our children play on. Sometimes they star, sometimes they don't. But they all capture the feeling shared by a friend's son as she told us of the team he played on. For the season's nine games he stood, immobile, three feet from the soccer goal. After each game the mother and father would pat the boy on the back and say, "Great game, son." The boy's eyes would shine with happiness as he experienced his first season's team experience. Finally on the last game the boy caught the message of the soccer game, and instead of standing perfectly still the entire game, he took off and began running with the other boys. When the game was over the boy was first to say to his parents, "Wasn't that a great game?" He had experienced the inner joy of participation with his family supporting him all the way.

Church athletic programs give families the opportunity to do things together. Our ward captured a berth in the regional softball tournament one summer. In fact, we terminated our summer vacation two days early so we could participate. What a thrill it was to have four teenage daughters involved on that winning team! As each one succeeded in performing to the best of her ability, we felt a tinge of embarrassment entwined with pride as the scorekeeper read out four Madsen names in a row. First Kristin hit a single; then Annette hit a single, getting Kristin to second base. Melissa was intentionally walked, which loaded the bases with Madsens. Then Suzanne, the fourth Madsen to be up to bat in a row, hit a grand slam home run. Hooray! That's joy!

Music also gives families an opportunity to do things together, and can create feelings of happiness. The contribution one makes to a chamber ensemble, symphony orchestra, or band gives one somewhat the same feelings a football or basketball player experiences as he contributes to his team's efforts. Everyone in the family can participate in musical endeavors. As the children practice to perfect their musical talents, the parents can also practice.

After a twenty-year absence from playing in college

musical groups, I have recently performed in a community orchestra. I have delighted in the challenge of improving my talents with the support of my family encouraging me on. Without their help I would not have been able to leave our home for the weekly rehearsals. The family has thus seen how important it is for everyone, whether mother, father, teenagers, or children, to be able to pursue something that is important for his own personal joy. Encouraging children to study music gives them not only appreciation for some of the finer things of life, but also the opportunity to serve others. It's neat to have a son or daughter be the Primary organist, or the song leader at activity night.

But as with any diversion from usual activity, when practice time comes around each day, there are bound to be excuses arise, or a sudden lack of enthusiasm. When cross words begin to abound, and negativism, it is normal to ask oneself, "Is it worth it?" It could be all-consuming to make sure that one child did his required amount of practice time daily, let alone six or eight. There are so many other things that need attention during the day that it is easy for discouragement to creep in. Surely it would be much easier not to have the children involved in any lessons.

Persistent effort is worth the price, however, as we rediscovered one evening. My four older daughters and I were asked to perform the musical score for a leadership program in our stake. We were not only to play our musical instruments, but also to sing four or five songs. The practice sessions became heated more than once, but when the final dress rehearsal ended, we all knew that we had just experienced a beautiful kind of joy. Following the performance one daughter expressed our feelings in performing when she said, "We're sure not the Lennon Sisters. We are the Lemon Sisters." We knew we were not competition for any reigning musical group, but because of our struggle in continued practice with our talents and being willing to give of our music when asked, we felt the inner joy that can come from doing things together. As we produce familiar strains from our family orchestra, now consisting of four violins, one viola, a flute, a clarinet, a piano, and various rhythm instruments, we all realize the satisfaction that comes from practicing.

I would highly recommend attending local recitals, children's ballet theater, community concerts, and art shows together. School concerts of family members are some of the most enjoyable concerts one will attend. Children gain an understanding and appreciation for music when they are brought up supporting other brothers and sisters in their musical endeavors. And each one performs better knowing the family is there to cheer him or her on.

As the vision is enlarged, it makes one day's work to pay the price of a symphony concert or to buy a special oil painting well worth the price. Until then, joy is realized when the three-year-old sings at the top of his lungs, "Jingle bells, jingle bells, jingle all the way" over and over and over for ten minutes straight. It's also a test of patient endurance for the listeners!

We like to do things together. We enjoy each other's company. It's as much fun for an older brother to take a little sister exploring in the mountain trails behind our home as it is to ride bicycles over to the school and back. We like going to Grandma's house to swim as much as we like going to a movie. Reading Book of Mormon stories with younger children at bedtime is rewarding. The daily or Sunday night practice of scripture reading with the older members of the family can give many opportunities for important discussions and thought-provoking questions. Our children look forward to their eighth birthday, for they know they will receive a special Bible from their grandparents. Scripture reading is much more interesting when one has his own scriptures to read and mark. No family home evening lesson is learned as well as the one that the child prepares himself. The lessons learned are better than continual lectures from parents. We like to always conclude a family home evening lesson by giving three "hip-hip-hoorays" for the lesson giver.

Sometimes it's hard to do things always together, either because of a time element or because it involves learning new skills, or performing at a faster pace than one is accustomed to. Age differences are contributing factors also. But as we practice and persist we know that "families are to have joy."

My father taught us children that the first and great law of heaven was and is obedience. As he is now preparing to enter great-grandfatherhood I am sure that he will leave this lesson with great-grandchildren as well. Obedience is necessary to experience the freedom of joyful feelings. Obedience may mean not always doing what we want to do, but bending our will at times to do what is asked of us, or to do what the majority wants, or what the parents think is best for the entire family. Obedience involves giving of ourselves for others, such as teaching that Primary class when school assignments demand extra time for studying and we're really too busy. Obedience means missing the family trip that we are already packed for because stake conference is unexpectedly moved up one week. Obedience encompasses loyalty to one another's commitments. It is honoring the private time of another family member. Obedience is playing ball in our backyard with the neighborhood gang—and accidentally breaking a window not once, not twice, but three times in one summer—because the unwritten neighborhood law puts out the welcome sign only on our beaten grass.

We have a plan in our family that helps to maintain the order necessary for many different personalities living together. It is as simple at times as having the same assigned seat at the dinner table. This creates less confusion at mealtimes, for the entire family knows just where to go when the dinner bell is rung. The plan can become as complex as a jigsaw puzzle when each is assigned a different task to be performed at the same time, or at least before day's end. As jobs are shared in the home, the tired, cross, impatient mother disappears, and a pleasant person appears. The jobs could be rotated and could also give the doer an opportunity for choosing. I am reminded of the time our eight-year-old boy reminded me that he had taken out enough garbage, and he now wanted to do the dishes. Our children do not receive pay for jobs done in the home, not even for the hours and hours of babysitting they do. Instead they perform their tasks because of their responsibility as family members. Money is earned in other ways. Like it or not, living requires work. Beds must be made, meals prepared, clothes washed, bathrooms scrubbed, floors vacuumed, windows washed, garbage disposed of, gardens weeded and cared for. Obedience to the various chores mandatory in a home can determine the tenor of the home. Chores can be done with a negative attitude or a slovenly performance, or happily as we proceed to put into practice the word of James M. Barrie, author of the classic *Peter Pan*, when he suggested that "the secret of happiness is not in doing what one likes to do, but in liking what one has to do." This philosophy, intertwined with the "have-to's" of family life, can create joy.

Obedience involves communication. It is important to let other family members know of our whereabouts. Our daughter has a friend who never knows why she is being babysat. It is as if she is not important enough to be consulted or informed. We need to let family members know where we are going and when we will return. It is wise and safe. A telephone is usually close and can save a lot of tense moments if used when one is going to be late. One night my husband didn't come home from work on time. The children and I suffered undue worry, picturing him overturned in a ditch, being held up while depositing the money in the bank, hurt in a traffic accident, and many other frightening things. When he returned and explained he had been helping someone and was unaware of the time, he received a good lesson from all the members of his family on the use of the telephone. The dating teenagers were given a firsthand lesson on how one worries when someone is late. Opposition appears and must be dealt with.

It is necessary to understand that no matter how important the eternal family unit is said to be, or how much we do together, or how obedient to the laws of the home and life we are, true and lasting joy will not result without another very important step—preparation.

Alfred, Lord Tennyson, the great British poet, once said, "The towers of tomorrow are built upon the foundations of today." Any business, office, home or school that runs smoothly will have incorporated the practice of advance preparation. The foundation will be strong.

I once heard a beautiful soprano share her talent with a group of friends. We all clapped and rejoiced that the Lord had so greatly blessed this woman with such a beautiful voice. Then her husband stood up and explained to us about the long hours his wife had spent practicing, working, and sacrificing so that we could enjoy her lovely voice. It did not just come easily, as we might have imagined that night. This woman had prepared for years so that others could enjoy her talent that evening.

As we assess our lives and the lives of other families, we need to be sure to look beneath the surface and discover the truth that those who are happiest are those who have prepared to be happy. Our sons will know the joy of missionary service if they have prepared for it. Our sons and daughters will experience the happy promise of temple marriage if they have prepared for it. We will enjoy that special family vacation if we plan for it. We can't honestly be disappointed if the good things don't happen if we haven't adequately prepared. Louis Pasteur expressed it this way: "Chance favors only those minds which are prepared." Chance brings joy to those families who have prepared.

A newspaper article a few years ago caught my eye. It told of a man, age sixty, who had been asked to give a pint of his rare type-O Rh-negative blood to resupply a blood center's store. The man had complied, and the very next day he was critically injured in an accident that necessitated surgery and a blood transfusion. This man's own blood, contributed only the day before, was used for the transfusion. Preparation! That brings joy!

There can be no substitute for advance preparation, whether it is building bridges, earning a doctoral degree, playing a musical instrument, teaching a class, or managing a family. Someone has said, "To fail to prepare is to prepare to fail." Have we prepared to have joy in our families?

The Psalmist said that the Lord "maketh . . . woman . . . to be a joyful mother of children." (Psalm 113:9.) I read into this scripture that the family is meant to have joy. When one child wants to play ball, another wants to go shopping for a much-needed dress, another wants to get his bike fixed, another needs a haircut, another needs help with a special school project that is due *now*, another reminds us that we haven't yet checked last week's school papers, another needs help with her violin practicing, not to mention the little ones who simply need a little physical attention at the moment, and mother needs some quiet time to organize her thoughts for the upcoming Relief Society lesson she is to give, one might ask, "This is joy?" Yes! Allow me to share a dozen or so "joys" resulting from the aforementioned areas.

Joy has found life as two busy parents have awakened on their marriage anniversary morning and found the front lawn toilet-papered and shaving-cream greetings of love and endearment spread on the windows of the house.

Joy visits when Mom is awakened on her birthday

with a lovely cake baked and decorated and brought to her in bed by her children singing "Happy Birthday" and insisting it must be eaten for breakfast.

Joy is going to the hospital once, twice, or ten times to welcome a new little spirit into the world, and a sister asking, "Why don't they invent a new-baby-smell perfume?"

Joy is a family ordering at McDonald's in shifts because the waitress refuses to handle twelve different orders.

Joy is watching your children taking care of each other in diverse situations when just moments before it looked as if they would tear each other apart.

Joy is sharing the flu because you wanted to share your drink with your sister.

Joy is being kissed ten times, at least, after being tucked in bed, and being told the same number of times, "Good night, mommy and daddy. I love you."

Joy is the look on your child's face as he emerges from the waters of baptism.

Joy is eating vegetables in January that were canned from the family garden in August.

Joy is being told by a four-year-old that her daddy's real name is "Bishop."

Joy is losing the election at the same school where your sister won and having the winning sister cry harder than the loser.

Joy is finding your hidden candy supply disappear and discovering sticky fingers on your little brother.

Joy is having your daughter get her driver's license.

Joy is reading the scriptures with the family and having the two-year-old bring his own Sesame Street book to scripture study.

Joy is having your daughter and her date spend their special evening taking *her* little brothers to a movie.

Joy is sitting around the dinner table with the entire family and having someone ask, "Who's missing?"

This and much, much more is joy!

"Zion is built of perfected family circles," said John A. Widtsoe in explaining the importance of the home. (*Priesthood and Church Government*, p. 80.) I believe that as we actively participate in our family units, serving, doing things together, and obeying the basic law of obedience, our love for each other will help to perfect our family circles. Our family life, for the most part, should be happy. Families, the basic units of society, are meant to be joyful. "Happiness is the object and design of our existence," said the Prophet Joseph Smith. In preparation for this type of family existence, and as we face the recurring "opposition in all things," let us constantly prepare so that "men are," or families are, "that they might have joy."

Doralee Durham Madsen is an accomplished musician who plays the violin in Jay Welch's Salt Lake Repertory Orchestra and who teaches piano lessons in her home. A graduate of the University of Utah in elementary education, she has been active in the auxiliaries of the Church and president of the Brigham Young Granddaughters Association. She and her husband, Richard H. Madsen, have seven daughters and three sons.

THE JOYS OF
CREATIVE
HOMEMAKING

Winnifred Cannon Jardine

". . . and then shall ye have joy in the fruit of your labors." (D&C 6:31.)

Home is a woman's priority. She may not spend all her time there, nor all of her physical energy. But home and family have a claim on the best part of her thinking.

"There is no substitute for the home," said President Joseph F. Smith. "Its foundation is as ancient as the world, and its mission has been ordained of God from the earliest times." (*Gospel Doctrine*, p. 300.)

There was a season when a homemaker's work was thought to be scrubbing floors, ironing shirts, doing laundry, and baking bread. But her role has become one of management more than hard work. This does not mean that her job is easier; it is different. For keeping a family and home running smoothly and at the same time fulfilling one's own needs is without question the toughest management problem there is.

Homemakers come to their jobs with all degrees of preparedness. Some bring a knowledge of management and a variety of highly developed skills. Others, especially very young homemakers, have little idea of what their role should be. But available to all, educated or uneducated, impoverished or affluent, is a little spark of the divine called creativity, which is literally a godsend toward solving problems and making family life more enjoyable.

Women have more imagination than they ever put to use. Tests run by the Johnson O'Connor Foundation found women to be as much as 25 percent ahead of males in relative creativity! And a good thing, too, for everyday challenges of homemaking require decisions by the minute—patching a pair of bluejeans, thinking up meals and shopping for them, planning and planting a flower garden, making up Christmas lists and selecting or making gifts, getting children to do this and not to do that.

Making a home is an awesome responsibility because the influences thereof are so far reaching.

In the little West African country of Ghana, there is an Akan word, fidua, which means that the roots of everything that one is come from the beauty of the spirit of the home. The creative powers of the homemaker do much to build that spirit.

The Ghanaians say that a home should provide for the family a place where love and security and a feeling of belonging are nurtured; a place where mastery of self is encouraged and where one learns to make decisions and meet life on his own terms; a place where honesty, integrity, and fair play are caught as well as taught. (Virginia F. Cutler, *Home Science: New Horizons for Ghana.*)

Such a statement of family and home goals concerns the single woman as well as the mother of a family, for every woman is a homemaker. And the kind of home she makes is as vital to her own well-being as to that of her family. She absorbs from her home the attitudes she carries out into the world—to the supermarket, to her job, or to a church or civic meeting. And it is back to her home that she comes for rest and renewal.

If the home she has created can give her good feelings about herself, a woman is better able to help family and friends find a sense of well-being there too.

Homemaking is a two-pronged responsibility, dealing on one hand with the management of things (such as food, clothing, equipment, furniture) and on the other hand with relationships of people (family members).

Housekeeping, because its pressures are constant and obvious, often becomes the most demanding. And yet anytime the importance of material goods receives greater importance than the needs of the individual in the home, management ceases to be good. Housekeeping duties are important only as they contribute to an environment that nourishes the growth and development of family members.

Keeping a proper balance between the management of *things* and relationships with *people* is a juggling act. But creative homemakers do figure out ways of integrating the two: involving family members in the purchase and care of home furnishings or automobiles, turning the re-decoration of a room into a family project, assigning family members to portions of the garden to plant and care for, designating household members to be responsible for certain projects. Unloosing the imagination, one could list twenty-five different such ideas in a sitting, then try them out one by one.

No matter what else she is doing, a part of the home-maker's mind should be searching for ideas, answers, plans, or projects that will provide a harmonious balance to keep both the people and the things of a home in a pleasing perspective.

In managing the things or the resources of a home, there is a simple formula to use: (1) determine what the family needs and its wants are (setting goals), (2) assess the resources that can be used to get them (time, money, and energy), and (3) draw up plans for meeting the most wants and needs with available resources.

First of all, a homemaker needs to list what the members of her family, including herself, want and need. Because the list will include more than can be acquired, the items should be itemized in order of importance.

Creative powers will be taxed just to get family members to help make out such a list, and even more to get them to agree on priorities. But a warm, relaxing fire and a nut-filled chocolate cake are good (and creative) incentives!

Second, just what are the chances of acquiring the items on that list? A homemaker must take a realistic look at the available resources: time, money, and energy. Some families have more money than time to use. Others have considerably more time than money. And all have different amounts of energy. So each family will arrive at different solutions, but each will acquire the desired items only to the extent that available resources will cover them—and as the resources are extended by the creativity of the homemaker and her family.

Third, a plan must be worked out for managing those resources, for using them to the best possible advantage. Such plans are called *budgets*, a term that has come to mean something unpleasant; but it is, in fact, a positive and creative way of making progress as a homemaker.

Money is the simplest resource to budget, for while supplies of time and energy are limited, one can usually get more money if he's willing to work and can find a job. Many guides for financial budgeting are available at local libraries, banks, and insurance agencies. A homemaker should study them carefully and then adapt them to her family's situation.

Families sometimes feel that their incomes are so small that a plan would do no good. But actually, the smaller the income, the more a budget is needed, for every penny counts. Over and over one sees families of modest means but big imaginations who are in much better financial condition than other families of large means who have not planned.

Latter-day Saint homemakers require an extra measure of imagination and planning to include such added demands on their money as payment of tithes; avoidance of debt; maintaining a year's supply of food, clothing, and fuel; and the support of missionaries. Faithful observance of these commandments, however, once again brings that spark of divinity that sharpens management skills and opens up new creative dimensions.

The management of *time* is more important than that of money, for the twenty-four hours of a day will not extend—except as they are creatively used. Again the simple formula applies:

1. Determine on paper the available amount of time.
2. List those things to be accomplished.
3. Being realistic, divide the time available among the tasks to be performed, taking into account the priorities on the list.

Here, too, the creativity of the homemaker can make a difference, for through imaginative management she can line up tasks that can be done at the same time; or she can manage her days so that only one afternoon a week, rather than three, is needed for running errands; or she can trade skills with a neighbor so each is doing the thing she is fastest and best at.

Brigham Young once said, "Count the steps that a woman takes when she is doing her work, let them be measured, and it will be found in many instances she had taken steps enough to have traveled from fifteen to twenty miles a day." (*Discourses of Brigham Young,* p. 214.)

Management experts today call such a project a time and motion study, and recommend it highly for becoming skilled in home management. Once the steps and motions of a job have been counted by the homemaker herself or by an observer (two homemakers could do this for each other), they are analyzed and streamlined and then turned into time-saving habits.

Think of the minutes that could be saved by applying this to the regular morning routine of getting up, making the bed immediately, showering, dressing, and preparing and serving breakfast! Not only is time saved through the streamlining of the motions and steps, but also saved are minutes required to figure out which job to do next, and even the time required to overcome resistance to doing the job at all.

Just as the saving of pennies can result in dollars, so these small savings of minutes can multiply into hours that, used over the year, could mean a continuing education class or the refinishing of an antique chest or taking nature hikes with the children. Experts claim that creative time management can triple one's production.

Energy, the third major resource in the home, refers not only to physical energy, but also to mental and nervous energy, all of which play an important part in household management.

One thinks of fatigue, for instance, as being caused by a shortage of physical energy. However, physicians have found fatigue to be emotionally caused as much as 90 percent of the time. A study at Michigan State college revealed that the state of exhaustion among a group of women studied bore no consistent relation to the amount of physical energy they used. Rather, the amount of fatigue was positively related to the general dislike each had for the task at hand.

Frustration, irritation, discouragement, impatience, indecision, and worry are some of the gremlins that invade the mind and burn up nervous energy at a furious rate, robbing time of its work value. Sadly, the wrath of such thoughts descends upon the heads of family members.

Instead, let a homemaker's mind direct her in more positive directions: memorizing scripture, phrasing letters to the editor, improvising stories for the children, writing verse or singing songs, reflecting upon ideas for a birthday party or family home evening.

Abraham Lincoln observed that "a man is about as happy as he makes up his mind to be." And "the best stimulant to energy is happiness in a job," noted Lillian M. Gilbreth, management expert and mother in the popular book *Cheaper by the Dozen*.

Once launched on the wings of a happy heart, a homemaker begins to soar through work that was previously mundane—dovetailing tasks or systematizing them for efficiency, trying out new tools and seeking better ways of job performance, doing least-enjoyed work early so the rest of the day can be anticipated, setting intermediate goals with rewards to encourage family and self, involving husband and children in projects because it's more fun to do them together, finding joy in working for those she loves and loving those around her because she's serving them.

Harvard psychologist William James profoundly observed, "The greatest discovery of my generation is that a man can change his circumstances by changing his attitude of mind."

If creativity is important in resource management, it is many times more vital in human relations. And yet often creativity is used more effectively in dealing with the things of the family than with the people.

A husband may be skilled as an advertising executive or a wife may be totally creative in working out new needlepoint designs or making over clothes for her children. But how often do parents put their heads together to come up with ideas for bringing a child back on the right track? Or how often does a homemaker tap her creativity instead of her emotions to solve a marital problem?

Well-managed homes should have the involvement of all family members in their upkeep. But this requires great imagination and patience on the part of the home-maker-manager not only to identify the right tasks for each family member, but also to teach each one how to do the jobs well, allowing each to perform the tasks as assigned, then showing more appreciation than criticism for the finished work.

By devising games or contests, using appreciation and encouragement rather than force and criticism, rotating assignments and chores, issuing challenges, improving work conditions, providing rewards, and injecting humor and fun, a homemaker can not only increase the work performance, but teach responsibility and improve family relations at the same time. Such experiences provide happy family memories.

Relieving tense situations with a note of humor is a creative skill. And acting rather than reacting to an acrid word creatively sidesteps family confrontations.

Appreciation for the work of others in a family is a great energy booster for all. In a study conducted in Utah, over five hundred women said the reason they enjoyed doing certain tasks was because they received recognition and appreciation from others. (Rhea Gardner, *Management in the Home,* Utah State University Extension Bulletin no. 304.)

And what a blessing when parents in a home nudge their children rather than nag them. Nudging requires creative thought, while nagging takes only a tongue.

Creativity is not limited to those with wealth or education. It is available to all alike. The homemaker operating on a low budget draws heavily upon her creative talents to remodel last year's suit or prepare a tasty meal from a limited larder. A young widow working outside her home needs to use her imagination frequently to meet the demands of her job yet maintain close relationships and positive influences with her children. A handicapped mother digs deep into creative reserves to perform the simplest household tasks.

At one time I was a "scout" for a major woman's magazine, searching out home ideas appropriate for publication. Without exception the exciting and creative ideas were found in homes where money and space were limited and where the creativity of the owners was put to the test.

Correspondingly, on a national level, the great creative surges have often come during times of depression or national crisis, during times of need.

How does a homemaker tap the potential creativity within her? Geniuses have attempted to describe the process. Devote a half-hour each week pondering creatively over family problems, advises one. Go to your room, close the door, kick off your shoes, lie down, and pick yourself a creative chore, writes another.

One says that most of his ideas have crept up on him "in the middle of the night." And Robert Louis Stevenson spoke of his creative thoughts as "brownies," helpers who worked for him while he slept. These are the people who keep pad and pencil by their bedsides, for they know that good ideas are quick to flee if not captured.

A good long shower or hot tub of water induces ideas for some; exercise is a stimulant for others. Walking does the trick for one writer, while jogging does it for marathon runner George Sheehan, who carries a note pad and pencil along with him.

Dr. Charles Hobbs, a time-management consultant, maintains that good management begins with an hour of meditation and planning first thing each day.

Prime in that time should be scripture study and personal prayers. After all, the greatest resource of all for a Latter-day Saint homemaker is her Father in heaven and his guiding Spirit. She knows intuitively that the "brownies" referred to by Robert Louis Stevenson and the "butterflies" of British poet John Masefield are flashes of inspiration, whisperings of the Holy Ghost. And once she feels those special impressions, both in management of the things about her and in her relations with people, then it is her duty to have the drive to act upon them. If she will, the homemaker shall then indeed have joy in the fruit of her labors. And she "that receiveth light, and continueth in God, receiveth more light; and that light groweth brighter and brighter until the perfect day." (D&C 50:24.)

An author, home economics consultant, and homemaker, Winnifred Cannon Jardine has been food editor of the Deseret News for thirty-two years. A graduate of Iowa State University, she has been president of the Utah Home Economics Council and the Nutrition Council of Utah, member of an advisory committee on family and consumer studies at the University of Utah, and member of the Young Women general board. She and her husband, Stuart B. Jardine, have four children and two grandchildren.

JOY IN OUR HERITAGE

Claudia L. Bushman

"No man knows my history," reflected Joseph Smith. While it is true that the personality and character of the Prophet are elusive, many people seek to know his history, and his followers feel duty bound to seek out and learn their own. "We are a record-keeping people." We delight in the twisting together of families into ropes of related ancestors who stretch back into the misty distance. Ours is a vision in which we "save ourselves with all our dead." We are tied together, connected by blood and experience into a great human tapestry.

Perhaps it is this vision that makes us so eager to place each other. Are you related to ____? Where are you from? Do you know ____? These are immediate Mormon attempts to make connections. And almost always those connections can be made. "Oh, you're a Lauper!" people say to me, and I am pleased to be identified as a member of my wise and witty clan. I know people will think better of me for the connection with my relatives. Our missionary son, half a world away, reports that this exercise is played out endlessly, and that he is identified by his relations. The question is not, he notes, whether you can go home again, but whether you can ever leave. His heritage follows him relentlessly.

No matter what we are today, we can find things to be proud of in our heritage. Filial piety, or ancestor worship, has long been a part of our culture. Since Nephi began his narrative with appreciation of his goodly parents, countless others have stood in testimony meeting, tearfully grateful for the parents who have done so much for them. We have been scripturally admonished to honor our mothers and fathers, and seldom does anyone disagree in theory with that admonition. Such failures as we are guilty of we feel we owe to our own weaknesses and personal limitations, not to the idea that our parents are unworthy of our respect and admiration.

Appreciation of the family present and past is a cornerstone of our practical worship. We watch with interest as these values are adopted by the society at large. Appreciation of heritage is an idea whose time has come. *Roots* did not create, but capitalized on, an interest in families past. Young people were once ashamed of a noticeably ethnic background and wanted to be melted down in the pot and made more American than the natives. Not so now. They glory in their colorful backgrounds and seek to learn about and preserve their differences. Genealogy, once the preserve of antiquarians and the Mormons, has become big business. Why this has come about is less than clear, but fashion has decreed that interest in family and background is an important value of the 1970s and 1980s.

Although we are tightly connected to our past, we can choose a wider heritage. Heritage is available by birth and by adoption. The whole conversion process makes it possible for us to tie into a heritage other than our blood connection. We do not eliminate our previous past so much as add to it.

I saw this principle work during the American Bicentennial. The nation's two hundredth birthday was an event of such universal involvement, appealing as it did to patriotism, sacrifice, dedication, and every other high-minded notion, that it captured the hearts of the least interested Americans. All the nation was given a taste of history dished up in the most palatable form.

I happened to be in Boston at the time of the Bicentennial. Of course, Boston was central to the early action with its stamp tax riots, tea party, massacre, occupation, and the brief but incendiary battles at Lexington and Concord, where "the shot heard round the world" was fired. I was present at the reenactment of many of the Revolutionary events and heard plenty about those I did not attend.

I am not a New England native. None of my ancestry fought in the Revolution—on either side. My family came over much later. They didn't even make it in time for the Civil War, and they went directly west without stopping on the historic east coast or making any connection with colonial America. Yet when I saw the Bostonians disguised as "Mohawks" toss boxes of tea into the Boston harbor, when I stood on the edge of Lexington Green and watched the lobster-backs fire into the ranks of Lexington farmers and kill some, when I stood at the Jason Russell house where "the old men of Menotomy" (now Arlington, Massachusetts) crouching behind stone walls harassed the retreating English soldiers, killing some and dying in the attempt, I was greatly moved. History came alive and the war became my war. It was my cause. My revolution. And my America.

The American Revolution heritage is mine by adoption, not birth. But that heritage is legitimately mine. I am an American, and that is part of the common American heritage. I make this point because I want to make a similar analogy with the Church.

For many years the common heroic heritage of the Latter-day Saints was the pioneer ordeal. The pioneers were celebrated in song and story, and their heroic example was set before us to urge us on to greater achievement. Pioneer Day was celebrated in Utah and wherever a group of Saints could gather in July. When the actuality of a worldwide church with varied cultures and customs became a reality, the pioneer emphasis was speedily downplayed. Of what value was a pioneer celebration to Asian Saints whose allegiance was to gospel principles rather than to American mores? Even recently converted Saints in Toledo or Tampa felt left out.

But I think it is time to replay the pioneer scenario and honor the pioneers. They do provide a mythic example of dedication and sacrifice that is uniquely our own. What does it matter if our ancestors were not in the band? The pioneer experience is still a part of our common heritage as Mormons.

History is told in many ways with different emphases pointed up by different purposes. Heroic history, like pioneer stories and Revolutionary War tales tend to be, stresses courage and bravery. It is quite legitimate to present the past as attractively as possible, to make everyone valiant and handsome, but it is not the only way. Nowadays the trend is to reality, and faults are as endearing as virtues. Individual cases tend to be less heroic than the models anyway, and descendants are reassured to find that their ancestors were among friends when their shortcomings became evident. Just as we have problems, our ancestors dealt with difficulties. Such flaws only make their achievements more valuable.

It so happens that I do have an ancestor who qualifies as a legitimate pioneer—which means that he arrived in the Salt Lake Valley before 1869 when the railroad linking West with East was completed. Joseph Venables Vernon was my great-great-grandfather. But as is so often the case, his individual reality does not live up to the pioneer myth. His family refused to emigrate. His wife ever after considered herself a widow. Vernon came over with John Taylor and the sugar-refining equipment—which operation failed of success. He was a fine orator and a very dashing man; I have the account of a stirring speech he presented in the Salt Lake Tabernacle. But he had a falling out with Brigham Young and left the Church and the valley to live in Hawaii, where he died a lonely and broken man.

Though his achievement was less than triumphant, his experience has still tied me to the pioneers. Because of that connection I was able to prove myself a genuine

Daughter of Utah Pioneers, fill out the necessary forms, join that sisterhood, and organize a chapter of similarly descended sisters in the Boston area. Group meetings provided all of us, and others interested as well, a chance to discuss early Utah life and to feel closer to our Church sisters who went before. The pioneer heritage belongs to sixth generation members and new converts alike.

Actually the Church is my heritage. I am of an indistinct ethnic type—maybe English or northern European. When people ask what my background is, I can tell them I am a product of The Church of Jesus Christ of Latter-day Saints. My four grandparents joined the Church in different countries and immigrated to Utah, where they met and were married. On my father's side one came from Switzerland and one from Denmark. My mother's mother came from England via Canada. Her grandfather was the sugar-refining pioneer, but that connection failed and she had little interest in the Church before a dramatic conversion experience. My mother's father was born in Utah soon after his parents emigrated from Scotland. So there are my grandparents—from Denmark, Switzerland, England, and Scotland—brought together in Zion to build the kingdom and produce children.

Neither of the families had an easy time. Farmers on hired land without capital, good stock, or particular skill, they lived on the margin of subsistence. The good land was gone. Eventually my mother's family went to Canada, renouncing their American citizenship in exchange for land. They had a bad time there too, and eventually returned. My father's family hung on in Utah until their sons were old enough to seek their fortunes. Both families finally left the Salt Lake Valley for the golden shores of California. When they left the farms for city life and small businesses, they began to prosper.

Again this is not a triumphant story. These people did not reach the valley and make the wilderness blossom. They were not gathered in and cared for. They suffered real privation and suffering before they achieved a solid financial foundation. Their bright children went to work instead of to school. They sent each other on missions. They struggled and endured, and then they prevailed.

While financial success evaded them, they stayed close to the Church. Just as the Church was the justification for their coming together, so it remained the cornerstone of their family relationships. When my father went to Los Angeles to work and sent home some of his earnings to help the family, his pious mother, fearing that he was skimping on his tithing, turned the whole sum in to her local bishop. With such an excellent tithing record, my father was naturally called on a mission. Though he had his doubts about the advisability of going just then, he accepted the call in deference to his mother's deep desires.

So the Church is the backbone of our family heritage. Just as it was the cause of the family coming together, so it was the main purpose of life. The family had returned missionaries and bishops before it had college graduates and professionals. Now the family has both.

My mother, an ardent genealogist, used to ask her classes what made an "old family." The students would answer wealth, land ownership, important office, and other aspects of local prestige. Her answer was different: An old family is one that keeps records. A family that can trace members back several generations and whose members live in anecdote and statistics is an "old family." The goal of achieving an "old family" is partially in the grasp of all of us. Certainly it is easier if our forebears have done a good record-keeping job. But all of us can manage the four generations suggested by Church authorities.

Most of us who belong to "old families" benefit from the work of family genealogists. We have had several in our family. On a recent visit west my aunt Viola Johnson of San Francisco presented me with a compilation of genealogical sheets from my father's family. The book, more than two inches thick, holds family group and pedigree charts for many generations as well as family histories for two generations and a collection of pictures. Although I have had all sorts of miscellaneous records around, this authoritative compilation has become my standard reference, and I am grateful to her for doing what I probably never would have done. Certainly this genealogical record is the basis for a family heritage.

Genealogists always describe their work with great urgency. They must get those names down and in. Actually, once the records are one hundred years old, they have usually been gathered in some repository or lost. And once they have been preserved, they will survive. Barring nuclear holocaust or freak accident, work on those records can as easily be done one hundred years hence. While we must carry on the past, our major effort should be to preserve the present for the future.

My mother used to issue an annual family directory of her husband's family, listing each family group with the vital statistics, addresses, phone numbers, as well as professional situation and church position. Each family member had a number indicating when he entered the family by birth or marriage. The directory, carried on since my mother's death by my sister, now runs to more than twenty mimeographed pages and numbers 106 individuals. Four generations are covered and we are ripe to begin a fifth. Each family is sent last year's record to update and is encouraged to note important events that occurred during the past year. The result is that we all have current addresses and news and feel closer as a family unit than we would otherwise. One year my mother asked all the women in the family to comment on how they wished to be remembered when they departed this life. After a rather bad year, I replied that I wanted to be buried at the crossroads and forgotten. Such a reply was

not acceptable in this upbeat publication, and I go un-
listed among those who want to be remembered as good,
kind, and generous. As in all heritage documents, this
one wants to show a better face than the actuality, but
how wonderful that that particular face exists at all.
Someday someone will write a master's thesis on the
series.

We have all been counseled to keep journals, and
while everyone agrees that this is a good idea, I suspect
that the instruction is more honored in the breech than
in the keeping. The people who feel very guilty about not
writing more often in their journals should settle for half
a loaf. Halfway measures are good ways to get down important events without devoting huge amounts of time to
the effort. We keep a family journal, noting important
family and worldwide events each family home evening.
Such a record tends to be factual and self-congratulatory
rather than introspective, but it is a valuable record that
spans many years now. Another partial effort is a year-
end summary with plans for the coming year. In our
family the father makes predictions for each member of
the family and reads them on Christmas Eve. Like the
great Greek oracles of the past, these predictions tend to
be opaque and open to interpretation rather than blatant,
but they are also suggestive in directing each person and
pointing out strengths and areas for development. Like
in-house patriarchal blessings, they serve as direction in
vital areas of life. Then on New Year's Eve we read last
year's predictions to see how accurate they have been.
The collected series is filed away for fascinating future
reading. Such activities go beyond preservation to creation.

While we tend to emphasize the words and numbers
of history we must also value and preserve the things. I
am the fortunate possessor of the best ancestor portraits
to come down through our family. One set of my great-
great-grandparents was photographed, he in 1859, and

she about 1865. The pictures were matted with maroon velvet and secured in ornate gold frames in 1869. They have come down through the second daughter for five generations and now hang on my wall as an example of filial piety. They will go to my second daughter, named for the pictured woman. This past year I came into another set of family pictures. These are colloidal chloride photographs of a set of great-grandparents. They were taken about 1880 and show the grim and stern visages that descendants are tempted to hide in the closet or leave in the cellar to mold away. These two, William Reid Gordon and Annie Duncan Frater Gordon, had in fact suffered from a century of dampness and microorganisms. The corners have rotted away and stains of several kinds mar the surfaces. There is no indication that the fierce faces, softened by some artistic erasing to give an engraved effect to the pictures, have ever been framed and displayed. But who can throw their ancestors away? I called the local restorer of photographs and submitted the Gordons to his care. Before long I expect another handsome set of pictures, respectfully framed, to take its place on our walls.

Photography is a great boon to those who would picture their past. Few of us manage to inherit portraits done by the Old Masters, but photographs, now in common use for more than a century, people our past with images. We should think about the pictures we wish we had—our ancestors in candid poses, pictures of their kitchens, the identified neighbors they lived near—and remember to take those pictures ourselves, label them, and file them away.

After my mother's recent death, I collected her papers. An avid journal keeper who wrote daily entries for forty years, an indefatigable correspondent who kept her family in lively letters, a musician with drawers full of programs and correspondence about special events, she left the materials for recreating her life as a busy mother and bishop's wife. She wrote a friend regularly for thirty years, discussing art, family, and events of note; each correspondent saved the other's letters. I spent a pleasant month sorting and filing and then offered this collection of materials to the BYU Women's Archives, which collects the papers of well-known and less-well-known women. My mother's collection will remain closed for a few years and will then be open to researchers. My heritage will become the heritage of mankind.

My sisters have been moved to similar activities to preserve the past. One has collected favorite recipes from the greater family and will reproduce them for the benefit of all. Another has begun to collect the many wonderful songs we used to sing as children. In another few years this information will be impossible to gather.

As well as preserving things from the family, I think everyone should collect something of interest to himself. Old Masters, snuff bottles, and silver napkin rings are all very well, but aside from the high cost, such items usually have little to do with the collectors. I recently read of a collection of clothing bought by a Japanese museum thrilled to get it. A well-to-do woman had saved and labeled her dresses from special events throughout her life. There was her graduation gown from Vassar, her presentation gown at the Court of St. James, her inaugural-ball gown. That the dresses steadily became larger and more conservative personalizes the articles. This collection chronicled the individual tastes of one person and reflected those of an age.

Another collection I was privileged to view was the paper-doll accumulation of a serious collector. The dolls dated from the eighteenth century and filled 150 feet of shelf space in a museum library. This collector also drew her own paper dolls, hand-colored them, and sent them out as Christmas cards. Another collection is that of a friend who has more than eleven thousand postcards of Delaware subjects—all different! These are personal and significant collections.

For myself, I collect domestic things. I have little money to spend and only get things that fall into my hands, but I do accumulate. I have objects of women's work: a hand wringer, washboards, old irons, old baking things, a toaster. I collect pieces of needlework, small items of fancy crochet or applique to show how women spend their time. I collect old clothing and have several beautiful dresses from the 1890s and things made in older fashions. I build miniature furniture so I can learn how things are put together, and I collect current paper dolls (and older ones when they come along) as a record of my age. With some luck my modest collections will be sympathetically treated after I go to my reward.

Some collections may be junked or lost, but most will be preserved. No matter how abstruse or specialized the work of sorting out the past, someone will come along who will value the work done. An act of preservation is its own reward, but more rewards come along afterwards. Whether we save the stuff of our own family history or the stuff of our wider culture, all will be cherished in the end.

Will we be remembered? Shakespeare devoted some concern to the subject in his sonnets. Can we make our personalities so vibrant that they will transcend the ages? Can we leave such collections of goods that all will bless our memories? Yes, I think that if it is important to us, we have it in our power to be remembered as we wish.

To be remembered, build. A college library is about right to keep a name on the tips of many tongues. A memorable and imaginative dwelling may do the trick, or a lavish tomb. But short of building, the best strategy is to write.

Again, brilliant novels or poetry are beyond the skill of most. Fortunately they are not necessary. To be remembered, what is best is a personal and detailed reaction to the world around. The acute observer who regularly records her reactions can write the most memorable of documents. And she can draw herself as she wishes to be remembered. Her family can be made to say, "She seemed to be a little mousy thing, but she was really a woman of drama and passion."

Another way to be remembered is to produce a fine family. Progeny was Shakespeare's solution. Through our children our own transient fame and beauty is perpetuated. In light of this notion, the common contemporary decision to have no children is cosmically devastating. To trade all of the future for a more controllable and self-indulgent present seems particularly shortsighted. The person becomes the last of his line, a pruned stub on the tree of life. Of course many people who did not reproduce are remembered today, but it seems a dangerous gamble. Many of us who will never have an obituary listed in the New York *Times* and whose demise will not be noted in the "milestone" column of *Time* magazine can have the pleasures and frustrations of children.

Do we want people to bring flowers to our tombs and weep over our loss? Then it behooves us to choose accessible and attractive places to sleep. Family plots have become difficult in these days of mobility and expensive land. Still, if family heritage is important to us, we should rest, as families, in traditional places. If we are to gather up our bodies at the resurrection and join as family units, the task will surely be simplified if our graves are in a particular place.

I have long suggested that the Church should add cemeteries to their available social services. After all, our interest in people ranges far before and beyond the cradle and the grave. Our facilities should echo our sympathies. Families should purchase burial plots sufficient for several generations. If the plots are not large enough, coffins can be buried on top of each other. As an extremely generous Christmas gift, my sister-in-law recently presented her parents and each of her siblings with two burial plots. If we are distant from our own children, at least we will be close to two generations of family.

Our family heritage, stretching back and beyond, as it does, can be a constant source of interest, pleasure, and satisfaction to us. As the current living adult generation we are the preservers of the past, the creators of the future. The family honor rests in our hands, and we can pass it on as a valued possession or ignore it entirely. It is always up to us to make our heritage worthy of perpetuating. We assess the value of that heritage. No one will question the value we assign to it. Our children will take their cues from us as how to feel about their own past. To pass on the rich life lived before is a heavy burden and a great opportunity.

Claudia L. Bushman has a bachelor's degree from Wellesley College, master of arts degree from Brigham Young University, and Ph. D. in American studies from Boston University; she teaches social history and women's studies at the University of Delaware. A cultural arts specialist in the Wilmington Delaware Stake, she was a founding editor of Exponent II *and editor of* Mormon Sisters: Women in Early Utah. *She and her husband, Richard L. Bushman, have six children and reside in Newark, Delaware.*

JOYS IN GROWING OLDER

Caroline Eyring Miner

Growing older may be a time of sadness or a time of joy. It is largely in the attitude one has about it and the way one approaches and uses this period in life. Aging is obviously and inevitably a part of every human life that lasts long enough, say, past sixty. The other alternative is less joyful, you'll agree.

Women are always dealing with recipes for foods, or health, or beauty hints, or successful living, or whatever. I want to suggest a recipe for the joy of growing older.

The *first ingredient* is a happy, wholesome attitude toward life. Two tenets of my attitude about life as a child, which have become my two commandments now that I am past sixty, are: (1) It isn't what happens to you but how you take what happens that makes all the difference, and (2) make the most of all that comes and the least of all that goes. These two ideas when lived may result in an affirmative, optimistic attitude.

I am an optimist, as was my mother before me. To mother, Caroline Cottam Romney Eyring, the small town of Pima, Arizona, in which we lived was the most wonderful town in the whole world. She marveled at the sunrises and sunsets, at the weeds in bloom, at the smoothness of the cacti where there were no thorns. Most of all, she loved "the dear hearts and gentle people." Every play she saw, every lecture she heard, every song was simply heavenly. She was without guile and without criticism. She made life a bluebird of paradise, even though we were refugees from Old Mexico and were struggling to get enough work to keep food in our mouths. The song in her heart made the difference.

I thank my parents and my Heavenly Father for my

favored heritage and environment, for I have known joy as a child, joy as a young woman, joy as an adult, and I know joy now as a mother growing older.

We Eyring children gleaned our philosophy of life and joy from the ancients of literature and from scripture. I quote a few platitudes from Egypt's Middle Kingdom, which I heard often: "Live an active life, doing more than is commanded. Don't waste your time. Don't be bitter about whatever may happen to you. Don't grumble over your own affairs. Don't be irritable toward your neighbors. Let your thoughts be abundant, but let your mouth be under restraint."

The following excerpt is part of a declaration made to Osiris in the judgment hall: "I have not privily done evil against mankind. I have not been idle. I have not made to weep. I have given bread to the hungry, drink to the thirsty, and clothing to the naked." It stays with me from my younger years.

I am stirred by these lines from Browning's "Pippa Passes":

God's in his heaven—
All's right with the world.

This was my morning song, and my evening prayer was expressed by James Stevens in "The Whisperer":

No thought had I
Save that the moon was fair,
And fair the sky.
And God was everywhere.

From the Bible's Psalms I learned the essence of joy for the growing-older years:

Blessed is the man that walketh not in the counsel of the ungodly, nor standeth in the way of sinners, nor sitteth in the seat of the scornful.

But his delight is in the law of the Lord; and in his law doth he meditate day and night.

And he shall be like a tree planted by the rivers of water, that bringeth forth his fruit in his season: his leaf also shall not wither; and whatsoever he doeth shall prosper.

The ungodly are not so: but are like the chaff which the wind driveth away.

Therefore the ungodly shall not stand in the judgment, nor sinners in the congregation of the righteous.

For the Lord knoweth the way of the righteous: but the way of the ungodly shall perish. (Psalm 1.)

The earth is the Lord's and the fulness thereof; the world, and they that dwell therein.

For he hath founded it upon the seas, and established it upon the floods.

Who shall ascend into the hill of the Lord? or who shall stand in his holy place?

He that hath clean hands, and a pure heart; who hath not lifted up his soul unto vanity, nor sworn deceitfully.

He shall receive the blessing from the Lord, and righteousness from the God of his salvation.

This is the generation of them that seek him, that seek thy face, O Jacob.

Lift up your heads, O ye gates; and be ye lift up, ye everlasting doors; and the King of glory shall come in. . . .

Who is this King of glory? The Lord of hosts, he is the King of glory. (Psalm 24.)

What profound enthusiasm for a joyous life! Hopefulness starts early for the best quality ingredient, but it can be nurtured and improved by reading all good literature, and especially scripture. What I am trying to say is that joy in the growing-older years is a by-product of a life of joy from the day of one's birth, and, maybe, even in premortal existence. One of my favorite poems on this subject is by Walt Whitman, "There Was a Child Went Forth":

There was a child went forth every day,
And the first object he looked upon, that object he became,

*And that object became a part of him for the day or a certain
    part of the day,
Or for many years or stretching cycles of years.
The early lilacs became part of this child,
And grass and white and red morning glories, and white and
    red clover, and the song of the phoebe-bird.*

And Whitman goes on and on with what goes into a
child to make him or her have joy in the growing-older
years.

And there were the deeper philosophical ideals of my
young womanhood years that my father influenced. "The
Educated Man" by Isocrates (436-338 B.C.) was his favorite:

Whom, then, do I call educated, since I exclude the arts and
sciences and specialties? First, those who manage well the circumstances which they encounter day by day, and who possess a judgment which is accurate in meeting occasions as they arise, and rarely
misses the expedient course of action; next, those who are decent and
honorable in their intercourse with all with whom they associate,
tolerating easily and good-naturedly what is unpleasant or offensive
in others and being themselves as agreeable and reasonable to their
associates as is possible to be; . . . those who are not spoiled by suc-
cesses and do not desert their true selves and become arrogant; . . .
those who have character which is in accord, not with one of these
things, but with all of them—these, I contend, are wise and complete
men, possessed of all the virtues.

With the groundwork laid for a joyous life from the
beginning of life, a groundwork that forms a pattern of
appreciation for nature and her wisdom and beauty, of
love for and service to one's fellowmen, of appreciation
for God and the universe and the great philosophers,
poets, and religious leaders who have peopled this
earth—one cannot but know the joy in the growing-older
years. How could it be otherwise?

The *second ingredient* for joy in growing older is good
health. I am not so blind that I do not know that growing

older has some problems, and many of them are due to ill health. We learn that forgetfulness is in reality not a necessary accompaniment of getting older, but is in many cases due to disease.

There are also white hair, wrinkled skin, stooped shoulders, but with good nutritious diet, with exercise in the fresh air, with good make-up, and even an attractive wig or two, these subtractions of the growing-older years can in goodly part be overcome or minimized. With an optimistic attitude, a pleasant smile, and a hearty laugh now and then, who is going to pay that much attention to the detractions anyway?

The *third ingredient* for minimizing the aches and pains and unhappiness of the growing-older years is keeping a journal or diary. I have kept a diary every day since I was married forty-nine years ago, and I recommend this practice for a number of reasons.

If you are going to write about your days, you had better be doing something to write about. A diary or journal is a little nudge to keep active. I have kept in my diary the accomplishments and ailments of the family, the trips we have taken, the costs of permanents, motels, food, clothes, and this makes for extremely interesting reading. In fact, of all my worldly possessions, my eight children covet my diary above all else.

It is good for me to read in my diary about the early years of our marriage, and about how kind my husband was that first year when I had a thyroid operation while I was pregnant. I had almost forgotten how much we loved each other, and the tender ways we showed it with our prayers together, our little gifts and remembrances. Just re-reading this recently made me want to sharpen up a little in our everyday actions.

The *fourth ingredient* in the recipe for joy in growing older is the maintenance of strong family ties among us many generations as possible. My husband, Glen, and I have eight accomplished children, all married and with good educations and professions, and with families. But they are scattered from coast to coast, and only Glen and I are in the home nest.

We miss them, of course, but we have compensations in their telephone calls and visits in our annual reunions when we go to a different resort each year to enjoy our condominium shares. We get together as an extended family in home evenings and listen to and enjoy each other's talents. We eat and laugh and play games together. Our mature advice is sometimes asked for and even taken on occasion.

My family is one of the greatest joys of my growing older. Our children grow older too, and more interesting in the many challenges that come to them. My husband and I have great joy in their visits. We literally "live again" in teaching and playing with our grandchildren, and even with their children, for we now have three great-grandchildren in addition to thirty-eight grandchildren. The old tree keeps putting out more and more new green leaves. I leave to the reader's imagination the endless joys of this grandparenting activity. The greatest satisfaction I received from being made Utah Mother of the Year in 1973 was the accumulated loving comments written by my family.

The *fifth ingredient* in our recipe for joy in growing older is to develop many hobbies and interests. I have now a number of hobbies that I didn't have enough time for when my children were at home, when I was on the YWMIA general board for twenty years, and when I was teaching school for thirty years.

One year since my retirement from schoolteaching I made a lovely afghan for each of the eight families. Another year I took oil painting lessons and painted a picture for each of the children to hang in their homes. The children said, good-naturedly, that I then went around visiting each home to see if my painting gift was duly hung and appreciated. If not, woe to that family for they wouldn't receive another of mother's wonderful works of art. Oh, well, let them have their fun. I have had much joy in making afghans and paintings for my loved ones. I have also taken piano lessons and have had unbelievable joy in listening to fine classical recorded music.

The *sixth ingredient* in our recipe is traveling. The Lord made a beautiful world with many wonderful people in it, and he wants us to enjoy as much and as many of his creations as we can.

One recent summer I went on three wonderful trips. The first was to Maracaibo, Venezuela, where 250 Salt Lakers served as ambassadors of friendship and lived in the homes of our Venezuelan hosts. We had boned up on our Spanish so we could communicate with our hosts, and that was a challenge and a delight. I even got my husband to write out a speech or two in Spanish, which I had the opportunity of giving there. This trip was very inexpensive, around three hundred dollars, and was most fulfilling and satisfying.

Then I went on a trip with the Brigham Young University to the Aswan Dam and sailed down the Nile River, visiting ancient temples and communities along the route. We also visited Israel, Jordan, Rome, Athens, Cairo, and Alexandria. To visit King Tut's tomb, the site of the great library in Alexandria, the pyramids, the catacombs, the colosseum, Jerusalem, and all of Palestine with the innumerable sacred places was sheer delight again, even though I had been to these places before.

After being home to check on my husband, who has in the past traveled with me but who had a stroke some years ago and can no longer travel with me, I got my household in order and was ready to go again. My husband supports me in my rewarding hobby of world travel. He gets along very well, and I am able to share experiences with him so that he enjoys the trips vicariously.

The third trip of that summer was one on Eastern Airlines called "Unlimited Mileage for 21 Days." My neighbor and I went to twenty-six cities in twenty-one days, which my son-in-law said should be a "Believe It or Not" item. I am grateful for the good health that permits me to take these trips, because I learn so much and am able to return to give many lectures and lessons related to my trips to edify and entertain my neighbors and others.

Recently I also went on a National Education Association tour to mainland China, which proved to be a most rewarding experience, getting to know, even if superficially, something about the nearly one billion people of this unusual and intriguing country. I climbed the Great Wall and visited the Ming Tombs among many other things of extraordinary interest.

The *seventh ingredient* in our recipe for joy in growing older is service to others. I have enjoyed serving in the Church with the Social Services with the Unwed Mothers program; serving with the Utah Cancer Association and being on the board of directors; serving as a hostess at the Church Office Building one day a week, which affords delightful missionary experience for we meet people from all over the world; and serving in my ward as a Relief Society Teacher. I also find time to visit the sick in my neighborhood and take them samples of my cooking, which I plan on improving in the future.

The *eighth and final ingredient* in our recipe for joy in growing older is the development of our talents. Creative writing happens to be one of mine. I have had ten books published as well as many poems and articles. I write best when I write about my family and my parents' family and the places where I have lived and loved and worked and dreamed. Have you ever tried writing about your family and your own life? You will find this an intriguing activity for your older years. In this area also, I am the leader of two groups of adult writers and one children's group, the Strawberry Jams, and I have served as president of the League of Utah Writers and of the National League of American Pen Women. I have had two books of poetry published and was Utah Poet of the Year in 1976. I also conduct a sonnet contest each year at the high school where I taught for sixteen years and was the creative writing teacher and sponsor of the literary magazine. I recommend that each reader try his hand at developing one of his special talents.

To summarize, the eight ingredients for a recipe for joy in growing older are:

1. Maintaining an attitude of hopefulness and optimism
2. Maintaining good health
3. Keeping a journal or diary
4. Maintaining strong family ties
5. Developing many hobbies and interests
6. Traveling
7. Service to others in church and community
8. Developing special talents to aid others

The mixture of these ingredients is a workable recipe for joy in growing older. Robert Browning wrote in "Rabbi Ben Ezra":

Grow old along with me!
The best is yet to be,
The last of life, for which the first was made.

And from "Ulysses" by Alfred, Lord Tennyson, we review these great lines:

Old age hath yet his honor and his toil.
Death closes all; but something ere the end,
Some work of noble note, may yet be done. . . .
Though much is taken, much abides; and though
We are not now that strength which in old days
Moved earth and heaven, that which we are, we are—
One equal temper of heroic hearts,
Made weak by time and fate, but strong in will
To strive, to seek, to find, and not to yield.

The test for each reader is in the use of the eight in-gredients for joy in growing older. I've tried it—and it works. Emerson said, "We do not count a person's years, until he has nothing else to count." Say to yourself, "I am sixty years young; I shall go forth 'to strive, to seek, to find, and not to yield.' "

Caroline Eyring Miner, who taught English and creative writing for thirty years, is an accomplished poet and the author of eleven books. She was Utah's Mother of the Year in 1973 and Utah Poet of the Year in 1979-80, and received the Distinguished Service Award from Brigham Young University in 1964. A former member of the YWMIA general board, she is now a hostess in the Church Office Building and serves with the LDS Social Services for Unwed Mothers. She and her husband, Glen Bryant Miner, have eight children and thirty-nine grandchildren.

THE JOY OF CONVERSION

Darlene B. Curtis

What a blessing to be able to say my life on this earth from the very beginning has been a joy in the midst of growing pains. I was so blessed to be sent to wonderful parents as the second child and the first granddaughter in our family. My brother was one year old at the time. It was five years before my twin sisters arrived. During these years, with so many aunts and uncles, I truly enjoyed basking in all the love and attention they gave me. Then came a sister five years later, followed by a brother three years after that. So there were six children in all.

I was reared in a traditional Catholic home. Never once could I question the love my parents and grandparents had for the Lord, as well as for one another. Rosaries, novenas, holy water, statues, candles—these were all very much a part of my upbringing. The family showed a great respect for the role of the priest and nun as well.

I attended a parochial school for twelve years and was very active in the Catholic church. I had questions about religion on occasion, but knew my home was not the place to discuss them, as my older brother had tried to do so; it would just bring about arguments. So I continued to live as I had been taught and was certain of one thing in the midst of a religion of mysteries: that Heavenly Father loved me. I so wanted to please him in all I did.

Marriage was very attractive to me. After high school I worked as a secretary for two and a half years. During this time I became engaged and was preparing for marriage in the midst of traveling and enjoying my independence. But the closer this solemn and sacred event drew near, the more empty and unfulfilled I became. Something in my heart was not right. I really did not want to consider religious life, but the more I tried to forget it, the stronger the voice within me sounded. I finally had to take the necessary steps to commit myself to Heavenly Father in this way, for it was in this decision that my heart was at peace.

Consequently, in January 1961, I was accepted into and entered the Order of Saint Francis of Assisi in Rochester, Minnesota. I was just over twenty years of age. One of my first impressions shall long be remembered. The Motherhouse is a large, majestic, castlelike, stone structure that can be seen for miles, having been built on a hill. As my family and I approached the entry, we were greeted warmly by two nuns, one of whom was my big sister-to-be. We were then taken to an elevator, and while we waited in the tall, dimly lit hallway, a figure came toward us from the opposite end. My big sister commented on the importance of this woman, who was the Secretary of the Order. We waited until she came closer and I was introduced to her. The secretary put her hand on my shoulder, looked into my eyes, and said, "I want you always to remember one thing, my child. It is better to be holy than happy." Then she walked off without a smile. I thought to myself, "I'm going to show you differently."

In June 1961 my older brother graduated from the University of Minnesota in mortuary science and married a convert to Catholicism. They went to Alaska, where he had a job in a mortuary. There he became friends with a Mormon. Within a year he was baptized. In his letter to my parents, he mentioned that one reason he started investigating the Mormon church was the reaction of Mormons toward death. I can assure you my parents would have preferred that he had died than to have him leave the Catholic church. There were serious consequences for him, for our family disowned him for years.

I spent twelve years in the convent, growing closer to Heavenly Father and laboring in the privileged service of education. I graduated from the College of Saint Teresa with a degree in elementary education. These years as a "special servant of the Lord" brought a certain amount of peace and happiness as I daily sought the Way, the Truth, and the Light from Heavenly Father.

In the meantime, my brother returned from Alaska to our hometown, separated from his wife. He was going through a difficult time, and even though he went somewhat inactive in his church, he never denied its teachings. We, of course, had little to do with him. I was especially grateful to be in the convent, many miles away. Meanwhile, I knew Heavenly Father would answer my prayers and show him the light.

From 1970 on, circumstances were such in my life that questions regarding the foundations of my faith were growing in number, with fewer and fewer answers. This was partially brought about because I was working closely in the evenings with mixed-marriage and other Catholic families who needed formal instruction before their children could receive Holy Communion or the Sacrament of Penance because they did not send their children to Catholic schools. Many of these people, whose needs were not being met by the church, were frustrated by the lack of consistency in some of the manmade laws that were affecting them personally. I tried desperately for three years to help this portion of the fold by attempting to explain the inconsistencies and to answer their questions about such things as changes in ceremonies, ritual, garb, age for receiving communion, and formula for confession. I studied Catholicism in greater depth. I also went to those who supposedly were in authority for answers to such questions and also my own questions that were evolving about such subjects as transubstantiation, the Trinity, original sin, infant baptism, prayers for the dead, indulgences, priesthood authority, and divorce, but was told more often than not that "there are many things that require faith, and someday we will somehow gain a clearer understanding of these things."

I was painfully coming to the realization that the true church of Jesus Christ had to have more than traditions and manmade laws that I was so much a part of. It began to appear that what truth was there was distorted. A great example of this distortion was found in the beautiful, committed, dedicated people who were living frustrated lives of abnormality in celibacy.

I was able to spend the Christmas of 1972 with my family. Up to this time I had not shared the feelings that were growing in my heart about my disillusionments with the Catholic church, for I knew the pain this would bring to my family, perhaps far greater than that brought by my brother. By this time he had returned to activity in the Mormon church and married another Catholic woman with four children, who were eventually baptized Mormons.

Time softened our hearts, and love prevailed as we saw the fulfillment that came to this family as they lived the gospel. Acceptance and communication improved so much that they invited my parents and me to a Christmas day service at their church. The children were in a skit, and only out of love for them did we go (after attending Mass, of course). Upon our arrival, we were welcomed by about fifty members. I shall never forget the women who came up to me and said, "Welcome, Sister Darlene, I'm Sister so and so." I said to myself, "You've got to be kidding!" I had no idea there were sisters outside the Catholic church. I was impressed with the simplicity, the spirit and warmth, and was especially affected by their countenances, for they reflected the image of the Savior. They positively radiated.

Shortly after this experience, my brother invited my parents to listen to the Mormon missionaries (just to be informed, of course). He knew that Catholic friends and relatives were bombarding them with all kinds of questions about his being a Mormon. I noticed, as I would come home to visit, that my mother sincerely wanted to know how to explain various beliefs of the Catholic church to the missionaries. I attempted to enlighten her as best I could, knowing neither of us was satisfied with my answers. For some reason I started to become defensive, and would return to the convent after visits home with a renewed desire to study further about Catholicism. Even though I was having somewhat of a faith crisis myself, the thought of my mother making such a drastic change so fast to a religion about which I was so uninformed was very painful. It was not long before she responded to the Spirit that was working within her. With my father's permission, she knew she must go forward in spite of the pain and agony of knowing that he wasn't considering such a step, at least not at that time. The evening she was baptized, I shall never forget. I was eighty miles away at the convent, and remember so clearly spending the entire night on my knees, pleading with Heavenly Father to forgive her and to let us all see the light. Indeed, this was exactly what he was doing, but I did not know it at the time. It seemed so dark. This great lady with simple, yet profound faith was baptized and confirmed in May 1973, knowing she would be alienated from many family members and friends.

In the meantime, I signed a contract to stay another year where I had been teaching. I spent hours reading material on Mormonism from the public library. Because it was written by anti-Mormons, I enjoyed it, but not to the extent of being satisfied. Up to this time I did not give any impression to my family that I was interested in Mormonism, even though in my heart I knew Catholicism was not the answer. I guess I was afraid of what I might hear. Unknown to anyone, I took a book entitled *A Marvelous Work and a Wonder*, by LeGrand Richards, from our home. As I read this book, page by page, I knew that what I was reading was absolutely true. There were times when the witness was so strong that in self-defense I had to put the book aside momentarily.

The 1973 school year closed and I spent the summer vacationing with loved ones, attending two workshops on prayer and educational trends, and had plenty of spare time to study, pray, and just "be." Somehow I became the owner of a few copies of the Book of Mormon and carried them with me, leaving one here and there in my travels. Toward the end of the summer I was able to spend two weeks at home with my family. Little did I know that my sister and her husband had accepted the gospel of Jesus Christ, and their baptisms were scheduled for the evening of my arrival.

Their background is quite interesting. My sister had been in a convent for almost three years and her husband attended a Catholic seminary for four years, preparing for the priesthood. In an attempt to prevent mother from joining the Mormon church, they looked into it. I attended their baptism and was impressed.

I was also surprised to find that my father had had a serious fall and was bedridden. I was grateful to be able to be with him so that Mother could continue working in a department store. Due to Dad's situation, I did not leave home. However, every day my brother would stop in to see him. We would end up having lengthy discussions about religion. I was becoming very informed and yet gave the impression of not being all that interested (so I thought). My heart became more and more troubled. I had a contract to teach for another year and felt I couldn't break it for many reasons. But I also felt I was being hypocritical, representing something I could no longer believe in. I became so desperate that toward the end of my two weeks, I asked my Mormon brother for a blessing. I didn't know exactly what such a thing meant, but I did respect that which he stood for, and believed he couldn't make me feel any worse!

It was at this time that I first met the missionaries, who assisted him with the blessing. From the blessing I received a special peace and knew that Heavenly Father was pleased with me. I didn't understand just why at the time, yet it was so important for me to hear. I was then invited to listen to the missionaries. I accepted an appointment with them for the next day, and that first afternoon we went through all the discussions. I could not deny that which I heard was true, for my heart was filled with a great peace. I also knew that it would be a while before I could take any steps because of my teaching contract.

I returned to my mission August 21 to prepare for the opening of the school year one week later, but it was very difficult to get back into the swing of things. I knew I had to confide in my principal. Her response was one of concern and love. She felt that as I became involved in teaching, I would have a change of heart. She made it known how much I was appreciated and needed there. I told her I intended to fulfill my contract, but that I could not teach religion, which included liturgy preparation and the Sacrament of Penance program with parents. She said, "No problem, we'll get you a substitute." My heart felt less burdened.

The next day I shared my feelings with my pastor, who was in charge of the school. I had great respect for him. During our visit he said, "It sounds to me as though a piece of paper is the only thing holding you here." I said, "Yes." He wondered how I would be able to live community life with my sisters for a year knowing that my decision to leave the convent was already made. I didn't feel this was any kind of a problem, as they were supportive, trusting, and accepting of me. The important thing was that I wouldn't have to teach religion. Besides, I needed time. His concern, however, was how I might affect those with whom I would be living in the meantime. I didn't know. The rest of the day seemed like an eternity. I had grown to love the people I lived and worked with, but knew I was being called to greater things.

Late that evening a special school board meeting was called, at which I was released from my contract. The principal and pastor came up to my classroom about midnight, with tears in their eyes, to share the news. My heart was bursting with joy, as I was so grateful to Heavenly Father for making this come about so suddenly. I knew it was right. I felt such strength and peace in my heart.

The next day I went to the Motherhouse, where I would break the news of my decision to leave the convent to the president of the order, another beautiful woman and friend. She was not there. Instead, I talked with the vice-president, whom I knew by name only. Tears were shed as she begged me to take a leave of absence for a year, since it was such a serious step. She said she could understand if I couldn't live community life (and that can be a challenge, living with numbers of women) or if I wanted to get married, but to question "The Faith" was something else. I told her I had never felt closer to Heavenly Father, and that I wanted a final dispensation from my vows as soon as possible. The paper work involved was forwarded to Rome at once. I received a reply within three months, much sooner than I anticipated. Since it was in Latin, I couldn't read it, but it was my understanding that I was released from my vows of poverty, chastity, and obedience.

The weekend following my visit to the Motherhouse, I went home to tell my family what had transpired. I could detect a spark in the eyes of my Mormon relatives, but there were mixed emotions in the others. While I was there, the missionaries just happened to drop in. When they heard about the latest developments in my life, they could hardly contain themselves. One of them was very moved by the Spirit and told me to sit down because he had something to ask me. He said he knew I had a strong testimony of the truthfulness of the gospel of Jesus Christ and wondered if I would be interested in being baptized within the next two weeks. I was speechless and felt uncomfortable because I knew he was right. I couldn't deny one thing I had been taught. However, I had many decisions to make, not to mention the adjustments necessary after being in a convent for twelve years. In response to my silence and shock, he apologized and said he was leaving his mission in two weeks and wanted to be a part of this glorious occasion. He and his companion gave me their telephone number in case I might need them.

I returned to the city where I had been teaching and planned to stay there for some time. I loved the people and wanted to be able to tell them why I had left the convent and about the pearl I was beginning to find in Mormonism. It was quite a painful experience to find that my friends were not the least bit interested in what I had to share with them. I knew they were frightened for me, but at the same time they were not concerned enough to just listen to what I had to say. This was a great disappointment to me.

Ever since I was a parochial school teacher, I had had a deep desire to someday teach in the public schools so I could compare the systems. I immediately applied in several public schools in that area.

Three days passed. It was Wednesday evening. I couldn't stand myself anymore, because I felt I was playing a game. I was so grateful and aware of Heavenly Father's help in moving the mountain that had been in front of me, and for smoothing my path to be able to leave the convent. It could have been much steeper and rockier.

I started to pray earnestly for courage and strength to take the next necessary step. While I was on my knees pouring out my heart, the heaviness and frustration that

I had been feeling vanished as I decided to be baptized. I felt like a bird trying its wings for the first time. I immediately found the card with the telephone number that the missionaries gave me, went to the telephone, and by mistake called my brother. It was interesting that the missionaries were at his home when he answered the phone. My heart was beating fast as I told them I was willing to be baptized next Saturday, or else I didn't know when. I actually made it sound as though I was the one doing them a favor (oh, how I have repented many times since). There was such a burst of joy coming over the wire that I felt I lost my hearing momentarily.

I was baptized by my brother and confirmed on Saturday, September 8, 1973. It was so special to have my father present. There really are not words to express the joy in my heart that I felt that day. I now have horizons I never dreamed could be possible. I have walked from darkness to light, from a party line to a private line. It was interesting to me that not one friend (nun or priest) called on me to discourage me or inquire why I became a Mormon.

In living the true gospel of Jesus Christ as a Latter-day Saint, I have complete assurance that God does live and that he hears and answers prayers. For instance, I remember the evening of my mother's baptism when I was pleading with Heavenly Father to help us *all* to see the light.

Within a year after I was baptized, my father suffered from a massive heart attack and was in intensive care for many weeks. He was being treated by four teams of Mayo Clinic doctors. During his hospital stay, he had eight heart arrests. The doctors did everything they could to give us hope, but things did not progress as they had wished. Even though Dad had not yet accepted the gospel of Jesus Christ, he had faith enough in the power of the priesthood to ask my brother for a blessing. From this blessing we knew his life would be spared and that he would be given time to experience a quality of life as never before. He was released from the hospital shortly afterwards as a hopeless case. Upon his return home, he enjoyed seven beautiful months without any pain, truly experiencing a perspective of life as never before. Heavenly Father called Dad home in November 1974. How grateful I am to have a perfect knowledge that we will be reunited as a family, for it was made known to me that he had accepted the gospel of Jesus Christ five months after his work had been done in the Salt Lake Temple.

Another example of Heavenly Father hearing my prayer the night of my mother's baptism took place in the spring of 1975, when my brother-in-law called from Omaha, Nebraska. As a career man in the U.S Army, he received orders for a one-year tour of duty in Korea and could not take his family along. He asked if I would be willing to let my sister and their little daughter come to live with me for that time, as he did not want them to be alone. I was thrilled to be asked, for many reasons. They were well informed as to the changes that had taken place in my life. I could already see Heavenly Father's direction in their lives, as they were in the process of compromising their beliefs by attending the Episcopalian church (she was a Catholic and he a Presbyterian). I found out later from my sister that she had had to promise her husband that she would not get involved in any way with the Mormons, especially attending their meetings. During his absence I tried to respect his wishes, and this was a challenge, as I had so much to share. Mother was with us on a daily basis, and whenever we were together we couldn't help but discuss the gospel. My sister just happened to be there. I knew the Spirit would touch her because of her openness and desire to follow the Savior. As the months passed she was being beautifully prepared, but did not dare to mention this to her husband.

In August 1975, thirteen months later, my sister and

her husband were reunited. While in Korea, he had met a Mormon who dared to live the gospel and who impressed him enough by his example and spirit that he returned to the States with a pure testimony that the Book of Mormon was true. We were also informed that they had received orders to the Tooele Army Depot near Salt Lake City, Utah, for three years. It was evident Heavenly Father was showing them the way.

In October 1975, I was able to get one week off from teaching to attend the last general Relief Society conference in Salt Lake City. I was invited to stay with my sister and her husband during that time, and was very impressed with their enthusiasm and knowledge of the gospel. I felt they would surely meet the right Mormons to friendship them and be a strong influence for good during their three-year stay. I also knew that I must return to Salt Lake City, as it would be my home someday. Within a week after I returned home, I received a call that my sister and her husband were being baptized that following week. My brother and I flew out from Minnesota to be with them on this glorious occasion. What a joy to see a loved one enter the waters of baptism and be given the gift of the Holy Ghost.

The last example of many I could cite in reference to Heavenly Father hearing my prayer the night of my mother's baptism came about two years later. I received word from my youngest brother and his sweet wife that they had been baptized in Rochester, Minnesota. Their faith was tried in so many ways. Oh, how they love the gospel, and what dimension and meaning have been brought to their lives.

So five out of six children and my parents have allowed the Spirit to touch their hearts, thereby finding the restored gospel of Jesus Christ as taught in the one true church established on this earth, The Church of Jesus Christ of Latter-day Saints.

The summer of 1976 I moved to Salt Lake City, desirous to teach Mormon children and to be in the midst of numbers of people who loved the gospel. One week later, I went to the temple, the house of the Lord, to receive my own endowments and further instruction that promises me life eternal if I remain faithful. I was also sealed to my parents. What a comfort to know we will be united as a family forever.

Shortly after I arrived in Salt Lake City, I met my eternal companion and we were married in the house of the Lord. What a joy to be sealed to a man who loves and honors his priesthood, who is my king and a priest unto God. He has raised up for me seven beautiful children, five of whom, so far, have been married to choice companions in the house of the Lord, and, of course, there are the precious grandchildren. I love them all as my own.

My heart is full as I reminisce about that first day I entered the convent, when I was told it is better to be holy than happy. This is so contrary to 2 Nephi 2:25: "Adam fell that men might be; and men are, that they might have joy." What a joy and privilege to be an instrument in doing the work for my beloved ancestors so that they can continue their eternal progression. What a joy and privilege to be able to have the Holy Ghost as my constant companion as a comforter, a peacemaker, and a teacher. How grateful I am to know with every fiber of my being that we do, in fact, have a prophet, seer, and revelator on the earth today to direct and guide us. I have a sure knowledge that Jesus is the Christ, the Son of the living God, and the Savior of the World. I am especially grateful that the joy of conversion is unending!

An elementary school teacher by profession, Darlene B. Curtis was a nun in the Order of St. Francis of Assisi for twelve years before she converted to The Church of Jesus Christ of Latter-day Saints. She is a graduate of College of St. Theresa in Winona, Minnesota. She is currently residing in Rochester, New York, where her husband is serving as a mission president.

THE JOYS OF TEACHING

Ardeth Greene Kapp

It was a matter for immediate attention, some discussion, and a little humor when the editor picked up what appeared to be a slight error while proofreading a catalog listing. The new manual (which was to become a valuable resource for teachers throughout the Church) was listed in the catalog as *Teaching, No Great Call*. Was it possible that just two missing letters could make such a difference in meaning? No time was wasted in making the simple correction. The accurate title now read *Teaching, No Greater Call*.

While this error was quickly resolved, a much more difficult and important challenge would be to make the same correction in the heart and mind of anyone having the impression that teaching is "no great call." Yet that serious error does exist. "Just a teacher," some say of their involvement professionally, in the Church, and even in the home. And with that thought seeds of attitude are sown that, like heavy clouds on a sunny day, cast a dark shadow over what might otherwise have been a glorious time of teaching from dawn till dusk.

Instead of teaching being "no great call" as some may think, instead of it being "just a job" in the minds of others, the understanding of the joy that accompanies the sacred trust to teach is reserved for those who discover that teaching *is* more than a job. Teaching extends far beyond the responsibility to disseminate information, facts, theories, and knowledge. That alone makes teaching a job. But it is usually as one is absorbed in instructing that the joy of teaching bursts open like fireworks exploding into magnificent flashes of color, illuminating the heavens. Similarly, the student, while persistently struggling through the darkness in the quest for learning, suddenly experiences a glorious burst of insight and knowledge.

For Jeff there were hours and hours of constant encouragement by his teacher while he tried to understand for himself the difficult process of long division. Page after page of newsprint was covered on both sides by "just one more try." Jeff, with his teacher's help, continued the struggle to unlock the door that would allow him to learn this process. Tuesday passed. Wednesday melted into Thursday. On Friday, in the late afternoon while his classmates were quietly reading their favorite books, Jeff finally released from his worn-down pencil onto his very smudgy paper some numbers that for the first time, for him, made sense. In an explosion of ecstasy he burst forth with words never before spoken by this timid, yet persistent child: "Hey, I'm not dumb after all!" Everyone looked up, and for the teacher, at least, it was like beautiful, colorful fireworks bursting forth in a darkened sky.

On another day Julie squinted her eyes with her little face turned upward as if trying harder to hear and understand what the teacher was trying hard to explain. The teacher's voice was becoming a little more intense as she tried yet another way to explain what she had already gone over several times before. I was Julie's teacher, and with little experience in teaching, I began to feel very worried about my responsibility to this child. It was as I stood anxiously over her—observing her shoulders leaning forward, her head lowered close to the page, the firm grip on her pencil, and the tireless efforts of this little child to keep trying—that the real impact of team teaching flashed into my mind. I paused a moment and pleaded silently, *Father, help me teach this child who is thy child. Don't let her confidence slip while I struggle to master the art of unlocking doors. Allow me to learn the ways of the Master Teacher while I share in this sacred responsibility of teaching one of thy little ones.* With that immediate and constant access to the ever-present resource of a divine "team teacher," I tried once again. This time the key turned and the door swung wide. "Finally you said it right!" was Julie's jubilant outburst. Her broad smile and increased confidence were reward enough for the time it took to finally "say it right."

Even the most difficult, sometimes disagreeable, and even heartbreaking job of teaching can be transformed into the joy of teaching when we begin to grasp the eternal nature of such a call. Elder John A. Widtsoe gave a wider perspective to our understanding:

"In our pre-existent state, in the day of the great council, we made a certain agreement with the Almighty. The Lord proposed a plan conceived by him, we accepted it. Since the plan is intended for all men, we became parties to the salvation of every person under that plan. We agreed right then and there to be not only saviors for ourselves, but measurably saviors for the whole human family. We went into a partnership with the Lord. The working out of the plan became, then, not merely the Father's work and the Savior's work, but also our work. The least of us, the humblest, is in partnership with the Almighty in achieving the purpose of the eternal plan of salvation." (*Utah Genealogical and Historical Magazine,* October 1943, p. 289.)

If a person has "so much the advantage in the world to come" because of the knowledge and intelligence he has gained in this life through his diligence and obedience (D&C 130:19), then surely one who assists in any way in contributing to a person's knowledge, reassuring him in his diligence, and encouraging him in his obedience becomes a teacher "in partnership with the Almighty in achieving the purpose of the eternal plan of salvation."

Bodies are born only once, but many rebirths take place as a teacher gently and reverently leads one to discover his own gifts and endowments, talents and abilities so generously bestowed by a divine Father, for which the student is steward. It is in understanding the eternal nature and the divine potential of the material with which a teacher is entrusted as she leaves her imprint in human clay that transforms a routine job to inexpressible joy. "We are the children of God, and as His children there is no attribute we ascribe to Him that we do not possess, though they may be dormant or in embryo." (George Q. Cannon, *Gospel Truth* 1:1.) It is this knowledge that lifts teaching and its rewards to heights hardly dreamed of in other areas of endeavor.

Teachers are allowed, on occasion, to assist the student in unlocking the door to a vault of eternal talents, talents that at times have been locked up too long by one suffering from feelings of inadequacy, discouragement, and lack of faith in his own ability and in his own divine potential.

In the fall of the year, a young woman was completing her student teaching in a third-grade class. She had been diligent in learning the mechanics and methodology, and by the standards of the academic world was an excellent teacher. Yet, in her heart she felt no joy of teaching —rather, hurt and often nagging discouragement and lack of confidence, like spreading aphids on a rosebush, were sapping her strength and hampering her growth.

We sat together at the close of the school day. The classroom was quiet, the children gone. The smell of chalk dust filled the air, adding a heaviness to the silence that seemed to be closing in. "I can't do it," she said, "I just can't do it." Tears filled her eyes as she bit her lower lip. I knew of her great desire to be a good teacher and her untiring effort to succeed, yet her confidence was so weak that everything she did was seen by her as less than acceptable. She had gradually convinced herself that she was doomed by failure and there was no escape.

The curriculum for this important moment had not been provided. As I listened to her, I felt myself reaching out, pleading for an answer. A thought began to unfold, and I found myself posing questions—not so much about her performance, but about the children's increased achievement because of her efforts in teaching. Was not Sarah doing better in spelling than she had done even a week ago? What did it mean to have the children crowd around her desk during recess and ask for "just one more song" as she played their favorite tune on her guitar and sang with them? Her troubled countenance changed slightly, with the hint of a smile. I continued: Had not a child raised his hand indicating a need for help to which she responded? On the playground that very day had not her voice blended with the cheering that brought Jimmy home safely in the winning home run? Had she not opened doors for children—many doors, doors that in some cases might even have remained closed, at least for a time?

It was in discovering the evidence of others' progress that she began to discover her own. During the following weeks she spoke more often about what was happening to the children in her class and less often about what was happening to her. The disruptive worry about her own inadequacies seemed to be gradually slipping away as she recognized her ability to help others. Some weeks later I received a letter from her. "What do you say to thank a person who has helped to change your life? You've pointed out to me things that I just always thought were part of me, instead of bad habits that could be changed. I know it's going to be a long process, but I know that if you've got confidence in me, I can do it. Thank you for a new life. You are the vehicle by which it was sent. Love always."

It is only through team teaching that the inspiration for some lessons can be realized, allowing the teacher and the student to be taught. "And now, if your joy will be great with one soul that you have brought unto me into the kingdom of my Father, how great will be your joy if you should bring many souls unto me." (D&C 18:16.)

Into the sacred realms of another's heart the teacher

must proceed reverently, with deep respect, and teach clearly and forcefully only truths to which the Spirit can bear witness. President J. Reuben Clark wrote: "The mere possession of a testimony is not enough. You must have besides this, one of the rarest and most precious of all the many elements of human character,—moral courage. For in the absence of moral courage to declare your testimony, it will reach the students only after such dilution as will make it difficult if not impossible for them to detect it; and the spiritual and psychological effect of a weak and vacillating testimony may well be actually harmful instead of helpful." (*The Charted Course in Education,* in Boyd K. Packer, *Teach Ye Diligently,* pp. 314-15.)

It is not in knowing perfectly the twenty-third Psalm and then teaching with great skill the meaning of each word that one experiences the ultimate joy. It is, rather, in coming to know the Shepherd and then reverently guiding another to that same knowledge. Only then is one privileged to take part in his work, which is also our work.

The sacred mission of teaching and the ultimate joys that attend—those most lasting, those felt most deeply—are often borne out of struggle, anxiety, and determination that is sustained only through unwavering faith in God. It is as a child is taught by his own mother that the moments of greatest anxiety can become forerunners to the deepest joy and ultimate ecstasy. It is in the inspiring example of Sister Ruth Yancey, as she has dedicated her life to teaching her children, and especially her son Steven, that I witnessed evidence of this great joy borne out of struggle.

In the first few days after Steven's birth, Sister Yancey and her husband began suspecting there might be something wrong with their precious baby, although he had gained several pounds since his 2 pound 11 ounce birth weight. The eye doctor confirmed the young couple's grave concern. Heavy doses of oxygen used to save his life were more than the tiny blood vessels of his eyes could stand. They had ruptured and he was blind.

One morning as Sister Yancey was alone with her little boy after her husband had gone to work, her heart was aching as she cradled him close to her. She began pleading with the Lord in behalf of her infant son: "Help me to know how to teach him, what to say, how to show him so he can accomplish each task. Inspire me, because I am your tool in teaching this special spirit. I'm weak. I'm uneducated. I'm unknowledgeable about what should be done. Help me to know what to do and how Steven and I can accomplish it."

With faith in God, this dedicated mother willingly and anxiously shouldered the responsibility of teacher and walked carefully into those first fundamental lessons. "We thought that when children got teeth they'd know how to chew, but they don't. Children learn from imitation, by seeing others chew. So I would put food in my mouth and place his little hands on my jaws and chew. Then I would put food in his mouth. He would spit it out or start to choke, but after a while he began to learn how to manipulate his jaws." Months later she realized the joy of that first accomplishment—he had learned how to chew.

When her son was just a little older, this faithful young mother had to prepare for other lessons, one after the other. "In teaching Steven to walk, I couldn't say, 'Walk to your daddy,' because he couldn't see his daddy. So we bought a little push toy for him that we called his lawn mower. He learned to walk with that. He wouldn't dare walk around the house without it, because he was afraid he would bump into something."

While the lessons were very difficult for the child, it was his mother who had to be willing to suffer if the next hurdle were to be crossed. "When Steven was two years old we built a fence around our backyard so he would have a protected area to play in, and I would feel more secure about his safety. The plan was good only for a while, until the day when Steven found his way to the gate. Day after day he would stand at the gate and cry." Sister Yancey told how she and her devoted husband together found the strength to do what had to be done. They bought Steven a little toy truck with a steering wheel and a seat. When he sat on the truck his feet touched the ground, and he could "walk-ride" the truck down the sidewalk. This provided something he could hold onto and something that would be ahead of him and protect him from falling in case of interference in his path. "The first few times I would open the gate and let him out on the sidewalk alone, then go into the house and watch the clock. I would tell myself that I must not check on him for two full minutes. I would force myself to let him be gone for two long minutes at a time, then I would run out to see if he was still on the sidewalk and going in the right direction. Then I would go back into the house and wait another two full minutes." Gradually, with faith, the teacher's confidence in herself and her child grew. Steven would go to the end of the block and turn around and come back. In time it was two full blocks. Without the struggle required to open the gate, the rewards and victory might have been withheld, to the detriment of mother and child.

In the events of those very early years there were also moments of great joy. About two months after Steven's second birthday, the Yanceys moved into a new home. Steven and his four-year-old brother, John, were playing in the living room while their parents were busy putting things away. Suddenly Brother and Sister Yancey heard "America" being played on the piano in octaves. Both came running into the living room. "We thought John must be playing the piano. But it was not John. We just stood there. It was like a miracle. This baby for whom we had concerns about brain damage, his hearing, his sight,

and all those kinds of things, was playing 'America' in octaves with his third fingers resting on the tops of his
index fingers on both hands just to get enough strength
to play the notes."

From then on young Steven could duplicate on the
piano the melody of any music he could hear. He played
hymns, nursery rhymes, popular music. By the time he
was four or five he could play almost anything, but still
just in octaves. "Whenever I played the piano he would
climb up on my lap and lightly place his little hands on
each of my arms so it didn't restrict me at all, but he
could feel the movement of my playing. It was so easy to
teach him music, whereas most of the things I taught him
were quite a struggle. We worked; we had frustrations;
we both had tears. Sometimes we wondered if we were
going to make it—like the effort to help him learn to tie
his shoes—but teaching him music was a joy."

When Steven was a little older, anxious to provide
maximum opportunities for this child, his parents
purchased a second piano. Sister Yancey, an accomplished musician, would sit at one piano and he would sit
at the other. "No matter what I would play, how big the
chord, or how long the phrases, he would always be just a
split second behind me. He would learn it and memorize
it as we would go. His mind is like a tape recorder; once a
piece is there, it is not forgotten."

During Steven's senior year at Viewmont High
School, he took a class in music history and composition
in which he had to orchestrate a song. He chose "Sunrise,
Sunset" from *Fiddler on the Roof*. He wrote the parts for
all the instruments in a full band—twenty different
scores. Together Steven and his mother discussed the
characteristics and voice range of each instrument. He
would experiment on the piano until he could decide
what he wanted each instrument to do. Then he would
dictate that part to his mother and she would transcribe
it on staff paper. Together they would transpose it to the

key of that instrument. "With his ear, having perfect pitch, and my eyes, we made a pretty good team. I couldn't have done that without him and he couldn't have done it without me. What a thrill it was when the Viewmont High School concert band played it for us. There have been many such times of great joy."

Graduation from high school presented more challenges. The ceremony was to be held in the LDS regional center in Bountiful, Utah, on a very large circular stage. "Steven wanted to walk across that stage by himself. His father and I helped him work out a way this could be accomplished. We took him to the regional center. The custodian told us which ramp the graduates would be using, and where they would leave the stage. So Steven and his father and I counted the steps from the end of the carpeted ramp over to the table where he would receive his diploma, and from there over to the other ramp. We walked through it together many times. His dad would guide him up the ramp, Steven would walk the full width of the stage unhesitatingly by himself, and I would be there at the other ramp to receive him. This way Steven would be getting that diploma all by himself. It was a very large graduating class that year, and the conducting officer requested that there be no applause. Well, there was no applause until they announced Steven's name—then the whole senior class stood up and applauded." Steven not only received his diploma, he also received a scholarship to Weber State College in music. "It was one of the proudest and happiest moments of my life. It really was."

For a young bird, pushed gently from the security of the nest, there comes a time for the solo flight, when the teacher must stand in the wings trusting that the teaching has been sufficient for the immediate challenge, and wings are spread in flight and there is no turning back. It was at the airport that Steven made final preparations for his solo flight. His mother and father, brothers and sister would remain behind. He had accepted a call to serve the

Lord on a two-year mission to the Anaheim California Mission. Steven grabbed the handrail and made his way carefully into the big jetliner that would take him away to unfamiliar places. "As he left my side I got such a feeling of peace. It was that feeling of putting him into the hands of the Lord, as the Lord had put him into my hands. I had done my best, and now I knew the Lord would care for him." Instead of waiting for two full minutes after opening the gate, this trusting mother was prepared, with peace in her heart, to wait two full years with less anxiety than the two full minutes had previously demanded. Much, much learning had taken place. "I feel pride in him, and sometimes pride in myself that I was able to help him. But that is secondary. The most important thing is the feeling of gratitude, even to the point where I'm grateful for those hard things to learn and to teach. Life could be easier and more pleasant if we didn't have struggles, but we don't grow much that way." This great teacher expressed her joy and gratitude by saying, "I'm thankful I've had the chance to cope with things I would not have chosen to cope with because we've all learned so much."

The Yanceys are still learning and striving and serving as they share their talents and gifts with others. At a recent concert presented by Steven and his mother, the attentive audience filling the hall waited with almost a sense of adoration while this saintly mother, refined through struggle, lovingly and respectfully guided her handsome young son to the grand piano. She then moved quickly to the organ some distance away and took her place. It was as though the entire audience were lending strength to that moment as they wondered just how these two performers would begin together the very difficult classical selection that Steven had announced as their first number. There was that second of anticipation, and then the whole tabernacle filled with the beautiful tones of piano and organ in perfect unison.

Later Sister Yancey smiled as she confessed, "It may

have sounded as if we began precisely together, but actually I was just a split second behind him. That's the way we work—he goes first and I follow." Her explanation sounded almost like an echo of years gone by when she spoke of Steven's efforts as a five-year-old. She had explained then, "No matter what I would play, he would always be just a split second behind me." But there was a difference now. He went first, and the teacher's work was glorified through another.

It was the Master Teacher who opened the gate, allowing each of us to learn the lessons, even the difficult ones, that would ensure our continued growth, allowing us the opportunity to reach our divine destiny. He marked the way and invited us to follow. It is as we feed his sheep that we are drawn most closely to him and feel his nearness through the joy of teaching.

Ardeth Greene Kapp has taught in public schools and at Brigham Young University, as well as in the auxiliaries of the Church. She was also writer and instructor for a series of television programs for the Utah Network for Instructional Television. A former member of the presidency of the Young Women of the Church, she is author of The Gentle Touch *and* Miracles in Pinafores and Bluejeans. *She and her husband, Heber B. Kapp, reside in Bountiful, Utah.*

THE JOYS OF CREATIVITY

Emma Lou Thayne

We'd been skiing all day. The seven of us, Mel and I and our five daughters, ages eight to eighteen, were the last ones on the hill. Snow had started to fall about three o'clock, at first faint shards of white, then larger flakes that became a soft curtain in motion against the black of the pines, then a swirling cocoon. The ridge disappeared, and the valley. The chairs on the lift rose like spiders on an invisible thread between poles that materialized and faded as we moved toward the top of Prospector for one last run. In the time it had taken us to come down, get on the lift, and slide off at the top, nearly a foot of new powder had fluffed over the moguls, sifted the plump rises into valleys, and turned the arch of the mountain into an unmarked wonder.

At the top, off the lift, no one said anything. Not a word. We all just stomped into tighter fittings of our boots, beamed at each other under goggles and over burning chins, and slid off the soft mound beyond the terminal and onto the mountain. No one led, no one followed. We all just came down, finding our own way, making our own trail, yipping and oh-ing and laughing, all together, each alone. The whole world was ours, new, white, without a mar or even a suggestion. I remember feeling my skis run like sharp scissors through silk, effortless, descent a floating, a rising and bending, my heels part of some mystic anatomy that needed no signal and answered only to instinct and inclining.

How the others were skiing was important only in my knowing they were there too, loving it, laughing, and being headily on their own. That some were more skilled or more daring mattered not at all. It was simply right to be there, carving around the fall line. It was being alive. It was doing what mattered in a private region, in a remarkably satisfying fashion. It was for me the ultimate in discovery.

At the bottom of the hill that some had struggled down on previous runs, we gathered to grin and marvel. It had been the same for each of us—an adventure in self-propulsion. And so easy in the doing that we couldn't explain it.

I think of our coming down that day as epitomizing the creative process. It may be symbolic of what I would wish for our children in finding their way with faith and relishing and individuality to whatever their destinations might be, as the poem that came from it said:

LESSON # 1
Ski here, my child, not on gentle slopes
where the snow is packed and the trail is wide.
Instead, cut through the trees where no one's tried
the powder. Push toward the hill and rotate
as you rise. No, the snow-plow holds you back;
it's slow and makes you frightened of your turn.
Think parallel. Stay all in one, then learn
to ski the fall line, always down: Switchback
skiers in their caution never know how
dropping with the mountain keeps the balance
right and rhythm smooth. Don't watch your tips at
all. Look past them at the deep white snow,
virgin as light, and yours. Just bend, release:
You, gravity and white will make your peace.[1]

That is what creativity at its freest can be—the finding of the right combination of impulse and circumstance

---
[1] Emma Lou Thayne, *Spaces in the Sage*, Parliament, 1971.

and then the willingness, nay, the courage, to let go and take on the hill with abandon and expectation.

The "hill" may be a household to run, a community project to muster, a child to amuse, a paper to write, a class to teach, a marriage to spark. The hill may be rutted or rocky, not smoothed and glazed with new snow. The time for the run might be late at night with a teenager just home, or early in the morning with a friend to talk over troubles. Others on the hill may or may not be colleagues or companions, and their paths down may cause changes not always planned or opportune.

But running the hill with an eye to finding the way that is unique and challenging, the one that feels exactly right and suitable, can grace the most hazardous descent with excitement and flow. This is the joy of creativity.

All this can sound, of course, hypothetical and maybe improbable. After all, how many of us in our routine kind of lives—with sinks to clean and clothes to launder—can expect days of coming down any hill other than the one determined by our address, status, or distance from social security? Who of us can put together very many days of floating down anywhere except where we have to be, locked into some time frame that decides our distance traveled and course taken?

Too often in a busy life, the creative urge can become a terrible source of frustration. Wanting to write, for example, and not being able to find the chance, can be like standing at the top of that tantalizing run, skis on, bindings secured, poles in hand. There may be new powder, a sunny blue sky, and no one else on the hill. The impulse to follow the fall line can be so overwhelming that when circumstances make it impossible to have a go at it, all other inclinations are muted.

So what can an involved, committed person do with that often devastating demon, the creative urge that demands like hunger to be satisfied? Perhaps three things can assuage the agony of postponement or provide a way to enjoy the waiting.

First, it is vital to recognize that life is full of phases and each one deserves attention. "This too shall pass" can be balm as well as incentive.

In an old diary, the only one I ever kept on a daily basis for a whole year, I found this entry. It was in 1963. We had five little girls under ten, my husband was a busy young real estate broker and elders quorum president, basically happy but often harried, seldom home, and usually tired when he was. I was happy too, but also tired with doing what I loved and knew very well how to do—keeping house. I always wanted a house and always wanted to keep it and what was in it. But on January 16:

9:45 p.m. Frustration! Mothering I like a lot and housework could be fun if there were just that! But the interruptions! I find myself envying a cleaning lady's life. Scrubbing the floor is all right, but by the time I get cabinets, furniture, woodwork washed, Megan changed and fed, Dinny's soap washed up, etc. (oh, that etc.!) the girls are home from school with other etceteras. Becky to lesson, Shelley to b.d. party, gift wrapped twice so she could see it again. Rinda's hair in ringlets for play tomorrow, practice part. Then Mel home, dinner on (him off on an appointment). Bath time. The day is gone and I'm still on my knees—I wish just for praying. Oh well, it's done and looks great—for today anyhow. But all day the wondering if I couldn't be doing something a touch more productive than scrubbing the floor. To top it all off, my Mutual lesson to give tomorrow is on "Creativity"! Ha! And me with not ten minutes to myself and that article. Oh well, dumb anyhow. Work on it some other time. (Later) Now 12:45 a.m. Time finally. Even the refrigerator asleep. Haven't done a single thing I really planned to today. So now I ask, Why can't I be a conformist, a simple 37-yr-old housewife instead of a disaster of inclinations? Maybe next week.

What would I tell my busy daughters growing up, both as young women still in school and as young lives hurtled into a dozen demands a minute, all of them wanting time for creativity? I guess I would say, "Maybe next week" can be an incentive just as much as a frustration. In fostering the instinct to write, for example, to put on paper experience and response to experience, it is important to remember that "next week" things may be very different. Children grow, circumstances change, lives are altered. I was forty-five before I went back to school for another degree in creative writing, and forty-six before my first book was published. In the meantime, the journey was full of love and learning that no school could have provided. If there were floors to scrub, there were moments of competition to revel in. If there were schedules to meet, there were always people to delight in. Nothing was unimportant. And along the way, on paper napkins, in scrapbooks, under the hair dryer and in the most random of memories, the haphazard recording of it all had kept alive the amazements of the process.

Time to do will not always be there, nor will certain people. But the dark and the light will be. It is urgent to pay attention to both, as they are. Treasuring the journey is what sanctifies the recording of it.

At the same time, second (and this is part of the first), as with housework, never underestimate the value of fifteen minutes. Somewhere in a day or into the night, there can be those minutes when something can come to life. It can become a habit to turn to the creative, in this case writing, to salve and enlighten and rescue. In whatever space there is, there can be the examination that says life has been lived. I can take time to write if for nothing more than to explain me to myself, to write it down to find out what I'm thinking. Just as ten minutes reading a day will take me through the scriptures in a year and change my sense of the world, fifteen minutes writing any day can filter that world and take me through layers of human nonsense like the shedding of old skins. That shedding can keep me well as well as alive. I can stay intimately in touch with the wonderful, exasperating, inspiring, funny, bewildering, aching, impossible beauty of being part of it all. And when the spaces get bigger, as I always hope they will, those fifteen-minute snatches can maybe expand to fit the size of my need.

One thing to remember especially, some of the most creative moments occur subconsciously, especially when at rest or thinking about something entirely apart from the project at hand. I must never forget to allow room for the inspiration called by names as diverse as the "muse" or the Holy Ghost. Sometimes thinking hard on an idea or a problem does not bring answers. Solutions refuse to come until a restive period, when they can ease into the mind as unexpectedly as dreaming. My mother always told us, "Pray at night, plan in the morning." I do. For any creative effort, I let the Comforter provide the comfort.

And third, while not many make a living from creative writing, anyone can make a life from creative living. In any traveling, creativity is the saving element, the difference between tedium and, if not triumph, at least enjoyment.

Some people do chores; others have a work party. Some children have to take a bath; others get to have a frolic in the tub. Some students hand in a research paper that is a series of quotations from experts; others tie the ideas of experts to some of their own and make connections to what happened on the way to school that morning. Some plod through a job; the lucky ones take on a project. It is the process that matters, more even than the product.

Two neighbor children, Danny, five, and Carolyn, seven, came shoveling the skiff of snow on our drive one night. Their shovels were twice their height and the scoops of white fell off before they hoisted them over the bank. From the window I watched the two and their impromptu labors. After a few failures, Danny gave up his route and simply followed Carolyn's. What she left, he pushed along, and the driveway soon was cleared as well as it would have been by one of their father's snow blowers. I went out with cookies to say thank you. Both beamed, Carolyn showing me that I could tell her from her twin because she had lost all four of her front teeth and "Jennifer's just got one top, one bottom out."

"Thank you for the great job you did shoveling," I said, pondering whether to offer them more for their surprise services.

"That's all right," they said in chorus. And Danny added, "We learned how to be a machine!"

The creative process, that something struggling to be born, exists everywhere. The finding out, the figuring out, the joy that comes from letting it happen—that is creative living.

LuRae, a mother of seven, decides to take her stitching abilities to market. In eighteen months her husband joins her enterprise, and a family business keeps them and their children traveling and demonstrating, funds for the future flowing.

Kim and Janet like pets and children and find ways to build kennels and train Brittanies, Kim and his daughter getting them ready for field trials, Janet grooming them for show.

June, a woman of grace and refinement, turns an old house into a garden of greenery and refinished coziness. In whatever meantimes she can assemble, she touches her children with wise good humor and a whole community with betterment.

Elizabeth takes on a public relations department and makes of memos works of art and distinction. Everybody feels related and full of potential.

Megan, a high school exchange student from Utah in Haddonfield, New Jersey, nervous about playing a violin solo for the orchestra's spring concert, decides to play an unannounced hoedown as soon as she finishes her concerto. She is relaxed, and easterners clap and stomp to the unexpected beat of the west.

Sherry, a lover of color and design, builds a new house with a new husband, then invites a student sister and family of three to make an apartment of the downstairs and share the tending of their combined families so she can join her husband in an advertising venture.

Homer, a biophysicist, finds in analogies between computer data analysis and sailing the Straits of Juan de Fuca wonderful excuses for writing a book and sailing a boat.

Mike, a young attorney bishop, introduces at priesthood ward conference a skit about marriage, saying the trouble with women is often men. The bedraggled leading lady sings "It Takes Two" into the smiling sensibilities of two hundred believers.

Becky, a twenty-eight-year-old wife home with two little boys, teaches them to make their own puzzles out of cardboard as she designs and puts together stained glass lamps and windows for their rooms.

Joseph Smith, a fourteen-year-old boy, reads from James and goes to pray for answers he will make into a living force for good among generations he will never meet.

A complex and miraculous process, creativity may just represent the highest degree of emotional health of normal people who are, as psychologists say, "actualizing" themselves. It can turn the drab into the dazzling or bring what wasn't into what is. "Create" can mean "to bring into existence, to produce or bring about, to invest with a new form, to produce through imaginative skill."

But it is not the easy way. Creative living, like creative writing, demands action in direct proportion to the joy expected. It is always easier to go to sleep with the journal unentered, the letter unanswered, the poem untried. It is easier to read a story from a book to a three-year-old than to invent one to fit the moment. And who would not acquiesce to an afternoon of TV when there is a skit to be made up, a stand to be taken, a voice to be voiced, an idea to be explored—in writing? It is darned hard work. Full of inspiration and inclination, yes, but also wrought with perspiration. Even when talent is tweaking the leanings, nothing is harder to start than writing. Jean Kerr, author of some of the funniest books and plays of the past three decades, says, "I hate writing—but I *love* having written!"

Indeed. Talent *talks*, effort *does*. But oh, the rewards! Whether a piece finds its faltering way into print and a life of its own, for the author very much like giving birth, full of surprises and a kind of mystical contact with people never seen, or whether the "thing" is simply something that explores and clarifies some private territory, having written brings a recompense that must be akin to the "it was good" feeling in Eden—not so much that the product is necessarily so good as that the process is.

From the beginning, the process has brought joy: "And God saw the light, that it was good. . . . And God saw that it was good. . . ." On every day of the creation "God saw that it was good." Then he "created man in his own image . . . male and female created he them. And God blessed them . . . God saw every thing that he had made, and, behold, it was *very* good." (See Genesis 1.)

Little wonder that we who were created can find such satisfaction in doing the creating ourselves. For each of us the creative impulse takes a different course, demands unique expression and effort. Without doubt the mightiest creative force in any of us is the need to create with God new beings, to be part of the birthing that gives life to life. I will never be able to decide which was the greater miracle to be in on, the birth of our own babies or seeing the arrival of the babies of our children. But to watch is to be let in on the secret of miracles:

*Sometimes there are surprises. He was big and had
spent time hiking mountains and using his power saw.
Of her they said She'll never be happy without her
studio. When they wheeled her biting on the hand her*

brush had held, into the delivery room they said to him
Get on the gown and the mask—over there—and you can come.
Then she could see only his eyes, watching, and his big
hand at his mask as she pushed.

This is how it works, explained the doctor, deftly
extricating the grey scalp that became lavender shoulders
and then a sleek tiny body mottled with something like
cottage cheese. He used a syringe in her mouth and she
began to breathe without crying and even her fingers with
fingernails turned pink. Here, you hold her, said the
doctor, snapping the cord in plastic and handing his
daughter to him. His big hands opened and then closed
around her, a cradle. She opened her eyes under fine
dark eyebrows and scowled bewilderment in his direction.

Let me see too, his wife said, sleepy now, raising her
head with effort. He held the cup of his big hands up
to the mother and kept looking down at his baby, quiet
as rocks on the ridge. Look, his wife said, laughing,
she has your toes. And sure enough. They were long and
flat and had spaces between them, but they were very very
tiny, from the bottom like pink pearls. She was wheeled smiling
to recovery and beside her he held their daughter
for a long time. They named her Grace.[2]

For all of its intrigue, that kind of creating has limited adaptability. Few are the years and seldom the chances for that cooperative wonder. But there are other avenues of human perpetuation. And they must not be neglected or made to seem less than they are. The need to be creative must be given rein and voice, never be denied. While everyone must spend a certain amount of time and energy in practical decision making, defending beliefs and

---

[2]Emma Lou Thayne, *Once in Israel*, Brigham Young University Press, 1980.

opinions, in the reverie of longings, fears, exultations, complacencies, suspicions, disappointments, it is the blessed person who gives time and energy to creative thought and expressing it. Only through this can lives be altered and days be made better.

Composed of curiosity and observation, this kind of thinking does the combining that makes all the difference. It leads to a creativity that is more than a hobby or sense of craft. It is what Jacob Bronowski calls "the fierce commitment to a personal skill that allows the ascent of man."

It is this fierce commitment to that skill that allows finally for real happiness in the one with the personal skill and growth for those recipients of its legacy. While needing to create can be spontaneous and sometimes unexacting, as in picking flowers from a garden and arranging them for Sunday dinner, it would be less than honest to pretend that another kind of creativity is not spawned only through dedication to acquiring knowledge, honing ability, and working untiringly at perfecting talent. And that dedication can be a benevolent tyrant whose demands are as insatiable as they are insistent. In one it can be the need to draw or compose; in another, to build or solve equations or make a poem. But joy can come only in the doing. For the writer, only writing can ultimately satisfy. Whether ditties for assemblies, skits for Mutual, songs for songfest, verses for funerals, words on paper for anything—for everything, it is what must somehow be done. Someone in an audience once asked author Truman Capote, "Why did you write 'Christmas Remembered'?" He thought a moment and then answered, "I had to."

Words thought out and brought out are an only answer. What is critical is that the process be granted permission to come about. The thinking, the sorting, the connecting, the putting together—only in the happening is there the joy.

155

There is the joy of coming down that white hill, cutting softly and surely into the fluff of new snow. It is the white page, unexplored, the unbroken expanse, sometimes dangerous in its severity, often rolling and easy, never without surprises or challenge. It is the place where no one's been. If others move across the periphery finding their own rhythms and crisscrossing and accompanying the course, so much the better. But the coming down is the wondrous solitary climaxing, the rise and fall of finding a singular way in the untracked being there.

That it can, that that white hill can be come upon at all, the path down broken clean and privately, the arrivals along the way savored, and the finish exulted in—that is the glory peculiar to creativity. The mystic coming about is without question one of the greatest "goods" provided by the Creator, who knew all there was to know about the joy of having made something that wasn't into something that is. It is called being alive.

Emma Lou Thayne is a writer and poet, tennis champion, teacher, mother, and homemaker. She has bachelor's and master's degrees from the University of Utah and has taught English and creative writing classes. Active in civic affairs, she is on the board of directors of the Deseret News Publishing Company. She and her husband, Melvin E. Thayne, have five daughters.

THE JOYS
OF LIVING
WITH BOOKS

Marilyn Arnold

          I can remember as a youngster hearing my mother say, "Well, I can go to bed now. I've learned something." To a neighbor who might have been within earshot, that remark was probably puzzling, but it was no mystery to mother's children. One of her repeated admonitions, along with "Wipe your feet" and "Eat your asparagus," was "Don't go to bed until you've learned something new." I'm sure that many days she was just plain glad to see us go to bed, with or without a new gem of knowledge furrowed into our brains; but her notion, at least, was a good one. A professional teacher most of her adult life, my mother knew the value of learning. She had seen it light the lives of countless little scholars who had filed through her classrooms over the years, and she wanted her own children to hunger for it.

    In my childhood, books were precious things to be loved and treasured. Christmas always meant books, as well as the usual assortment of toys and trinkets. In the summer, though we kids romped and played with balls and teddy bears and cap pistols through every day, we always wound things up at bedtime with stories and books. And long before I could even read very well, I remember that one of my particular assignments during spring housecleaning was to remove every book from the glass-doored bookcases in our living room and dust it carefully. It was a task that I regarded with a certain reverence, and I probably took far much more time at it than the job required. I recall the excitement of holding again books I had almost forgotten about, of reading old inscriptions in faint ink—"Henry Lynn Arnold, 1920, Lark, Utah." My father. But the handwriting was strange.

And there were mother's high school and college year-books, the highlight of my annual excursion through the bookshelves. Who was that beautiful young woman with the soft face and black wavy hair? Had not my mother always been just my mother? The caption said "Rhoda Jane Clark." Hadn't she always been Rhoda C. Arnold?

I can still remember the titles of some of the other books: *Illustrious Americans, Heart Throbs, Ethelbert Hubbard's Scrapbook, The Man Nobody Knows, Popular Science Library, A Comprehensive History of the Church, English Grammar, Deseret Sunday School Songs.* I have quite a different set of titles on my own bookshelves today, but I have never lost my taste for those old and dear books of my childhood. Perhaps the point of all of this personal reminiscing is that for me, the joy of learning is the joy of books. There are, of course, many ways to learn—through observation, through experience, through inspiration, through pictures, through sound, and so on. But I believe that learning to love books is the first step in understanding what it is to be a human being in this world. Language is at the heart of human experience. It is what we think with, it is what we touch others with, it is what we pray with.

There are those who suggest that we should read books for the same reason that we take medicine, because they are "good for us," as if we had to justify reading at all. There are those who determine to read a certain designated number of pages per day, as if a book were something to be got through, like a stack of dirty dishes. There are teachers who give students "points" for every book they consume, never pausing to learn whether or not the books also consumed their readers. Reading books this way is to be a little too much like scorekeeping. Some years I read a lot of books; some years I read a few books a lot of times. Some people read faithfully down the best-seller lists, refusing to open a book that has not passed some kind of marketing test. Me? I like to browse on sales tables, and in used-book stores, and along library shelves. Or I like to pick a writer and ramble through everything he or she wrote.

Oh yes, I served my term as a competitive reader, watching the gold stars pile up behind my name on the teacher's charts, discussing the very "in" books at social gatherings, fighting sleep to keep my one-hundred-pages-a-day average going. Then one day I remembered something Henry David Thoreau said in *Walden:* "What news! how much more important to know what that is which was never old!" I also remembered that as a very young child I had known books as friends to love, not as enemies to conquer or medicines to be choked down. It does not matter who wrote a book, if you love it. Or when it was written, if it speaks to your heart. Or who recommends it, if it is true. It also does not matter how long it takes you to read it, or how many questions it leaves unanswered. Happiness is not necessarily knowing all of the answers; it can be knowing some of the questions.

We can discover many things in books, and one of those things is another human being, the writer. Walt Whitman, that great poet-prophet of democracy who wanted to embrace and love every aspect of his country and teach his readers to do the same, said of his own work: "Camerado! This is no book; / Who touches this, touches a man." And he said it did not matter if we did not understand all that he had to say; some things, after all, are comprehended only at an intuitive level. He insisted, too, that he would be "good health" to his readers, but not in the sense that medicine promises good health.

Another thing we can discover in books is ourselves. Books are mass produced and mass distributed, but most of them are written by one person, one word at a time. And that one person speaks to every reader one at a time. Reading is really a conversation between two people, and no attentive reader can leave such a conversation without having learned something about himself or herself. It is the books that have spoken to me in a highly personal way that I cannot forget. It is to them that I keep returning over the years. And surprisingly, these books are not always classics in the traditional sense. (Much as I love *Paradise Lost* and *King Lear* and a host of other mighty works, they perhaps are not quite mine yet. Maybe for still another twenty years, I will knock at their door with an awe I cannot describe.)

One of the books that has become mine is *Walden*, at least parts of it. Henry David Thoreau, even more than Whitman, is "good health" to me. Gifted with a subtle sense of humor and a generous portion of cantankerousness, Thoreau needles me about having too many clothes, and too rich a diet, and too many furnishings in my house. To prove that we humans could simplify our lives and live without becoming slaves to luxuries, he spent a couple of years in a cabin at Walden Pond. His activities there had very little to do with material construction of civilizations, but then again, his activities had everything to do with the spiritual survival of civilizations. He, as he said, hoed beans, chased a loon about the pond, watched a battle between red and black ants, chatted with anyone who happened by, and sat in solitude and watched and thought. His experience taught him that the real necessities of life are few, and that too many of us "starve" for want of luxuries. He also pondered the servitude of ownership and concluded that it is not we that own our possessions but our possessions that own us. It is relatively easy for us to write off Thoreau as an eccentric, for he was that. It is not so easy, however, to erase some of his ringing bits of prose from our minds. This is his definition of *cost*: ". . . the cost of a thing is the amount of what I will call life which is required to be exchanged for it. . . ." A price tag in dollars is meaningless; it is our lives that we spend. He says of nearly every material thing for which we spend our lives—house, barn, clothes, rich foods, and various other luxuries and adornments: "It costs more than it comes to." He chides us again and again for spending our lives for material things that we would have been better off without.

Thoreau also suggests that haste is destructive. He sadly observes that we rush our lives away, getting farther behind in the things that count as we strive to get ahead in the things that don't count. As he says in an essay called "Civil Disobedience," too many of us "lead lives of quiet desperation." But it was not only to prove a point that he went to Walden. He went mainly because he sensed that his own life was not what it should be. He wanted to get back to essentials, to find again the quiet purity he felt had blessed his life when he was a child. He went to renew himself and purify himself by stripping away the foolish superfluities, and by slowing the pace of his life.

For each of us, somewhere, there must be a Walden of the soul. For me, Thoreau's book is a harbor, a quiet place where I can mingle my reverie with his and reassemble the priorities of my life. Another such book is *Death Comes for the Archbishop* by Willa Cather. This book is also about a place, the vast desert of the American Southwest. It is about a Catholic priest who was sent to the New Mexico territory as bishop in a day when the only travel was by horse or mule, and the diocese covered several thousand rugged and desolate square miles. After a lifetime of service that tested his physical and spiritual marrow to the very limit, the aging man, now an archbishop, had been expected to return in his retirement to his beloved France. He finds, however, that he cannot leave the desert permanently. He finds that it has become part of the very fiber of his being. It was there that he discovered he was capable of selfishness, fear, loneliness, anger, and even momentary lapses of faith. But it was also there that he discovered he was capable of loving the simple and unlearned, that he could choose self-denial, that he could endure even though he was not heroic, and that he could count on God to pour out his blessings even in a seemingly forsaken land.

To discover *Death Comes for the Archbishop* is to reaffirm one's own faith through struggle and trial and questioning and the slow, sweet miracle of heart touching heart with divine illumination. One of these moments of illumination comes to the priest one cold December night when, somewhat despondent and unable to sleep, he forces himself out of his bed and into the cold to go pray in the chapel. There in the doorway, huddled in rags, is an Indian bondwoman who has been forbidden by her "owners" to talk with anyone or to worship. For nineteen years the old woman, Sada, has kept religion in her heart, and this night she has managed to slip away from her winter sleeping quarters in the stable and come to pray at the church. The priest leads her inside, and together they pray and weep. Then shivering in her rags (she would be beaten if she appeared at home in the bishop's coat) she shuffles off, full of joy for the experience of the night. Little does she know that the priest's gratitude matches or even surpasses her own. The illumination that comes to him that night is his greatest blessing of the Christmas season:

Not often, indeed, had Jean Marie Latour come so near to the Fountain of all Pity as in the Lady Chapel that night; the pity that no man born of woman could ever utterly cut himself off from; that was for the murderer on the scaffold, as it was for the dying soldier or the martyr on the rack. . . . He received the miracle in her [Sada's] heart into his own, saw through her eyes, knew that his poverty was as bleak as hers. When the Kingdom of Heaven had first come into the world, into a cruel world of torture and slaves and masters, He who brought it had said, "And whosoever is least among you, the same shall be first in the Kingdom of Heaven." This church was Sada's house, and he was a servant in it.

Another book that wears very well with me is *Huckleberry Finn*. Maybe it could be called something of a classic, an American classic anyway, but that is not why I love it and why I return to it year after year. I have read *Huck* too many times to count. Ishmael, Herman Melville's wisely naive narrator in *Moby Dick,* says that when he begins to feel "a damp, drizzly November" in his soul, then he knows that it is time for him to go to sea. But when the eleventh month drizzles in my soul, I know it is time to go to *Huck Finn.* Not that *Huck* is a soothing book—it isn't. On the contrary, it is full of the most serious kinds of comments on the way we human beings treat each other. It features liars, drunkards, cheaters, murderers, thieves, and even "good" people who condone and perpetuate evil out of deference to custom. But *Huck Finn* is also one of the funniest books ever written, and one of the wisest, and one of the most full of love.

Basically, it is about a boy and a runaway slave in the antebellum South who journey down the Mississippi River on a raft in search of freedom. They encounter every kind of evil imaginable, but they also encounter themselves. Huck has been reared to believe that human slavery is not only an acceptable human creed, but also that it is ordained by God in nineteenth-century America. The book is about Huck's coming to terms with the conflict between his training and his heart. In the course of the book, Huck comes to realize that Jim, the runaway slave, has feelings like other human beings. When he learns that Jim cares for his family just as "white folks" would, Huck observes, "It don't seem natural, but I reckon it's so." From that tentative admission, Huck grows to the point where he makes a conscious decision to "go to Hell" rather than turn Jim in. And for him, that is, in fact, the choice. He believes that God would have him turn Jim in, and he tries to do it. But in the end, Huck chooses Jim's salvation rather than his own. At the moment when he believes he is damned forever, we perceive that he is heaven-bound. He makes the moral choice, the right choice.

Huck Finn has so many wonderful moments that it is

difficult to choose among them. There is the comic seriousness of an observation that Huck makes about the Widow Douglas's objections to his smoking: "That is just the way with some people. They get down on a thing when they don't know nothing about it. . . . And she took snuff, too; of course that was all right because she done it herself." There is the debate between Huck and Jim about how the stars came into being. They settle on the probability that the moon "laid" them, because they have seen a frog lay "most as many" eggs, "so of course it could be done." There is the night when Huck goes out in the canoe and is separated from the raft by the swift current and fog. Once he is safely on board again, he decides to play a trick on Jim, who lies asleep, exhausted from the struggle to keep the raft from capsizing while he searches for Huck. Huck convinces Jim that Jim had only dreamed the fog and Huck's disappearance. But once Jim is convinced, Huck coyly points to all the trash that had swamped onto the raft while it drifted and asks Jim what all the broken branches and leaves stand for. Jim looks about him, then looks at Huck and says slowly,

What do dey stan' for? I's gwyne to tell you. When I got all wore out wid work, en wid de callin' for you, en went to sleep, my heart wuz mos' broke bekase you wuz los', en I didn' k'yer no mo' what become er me en de raf'. En when I wake up en fine you back agin, all safe en soun', de tears come, en I could 'a' got down on my knees en kiss yo' foot, I's so thankful. En all you wuz thinkin' 'bout wuz how you could make a fool uv ole Jim wid a lie. Dat truck dah is *trash*; en trash is what people is dat puts dirt on de head er dey fren's en makes 'em ashamed.

Huck is cut to the quick by this reply, and he learns a very important lesson about making sport of someone else's deepest feelings.

Everyone has heard of *Huckleberry Finn*, but there's another book on my list of annual "musts" that most people don't know about. Maybe I love it because it takes me back to the beloved fairy tales of my childhood. It's an early book by a now well-known writer named Eudora Welty, a little book called *The Robber Bridegroom*. It combines bits and pieces of every fairy tale one can think of, plus a vast collection of legends and folk tales from out of Mississippi's famed Natchez Trace region. It fairly bursts with bandits, evil stepmothers, talking birds, flying horses, vindictive savages, and severed but still conversant heads—not to mention kidnapings by the score and language so packed with magic that every page literally sings.

The Robber Bridegroom is full of joy and pain, delight and sorrow, as it traces a love story that is anything but ordinary. The opening pages set the tone for the tale, describing a stormy night at Rodney's Landing, a town that sits on the edge between civilization and the wilderness. I particularly like the marvelous figures of speech and the way the concluding sentence of this description tosses in a cleverly unexpected detail:

> As his foot touched shore, the sun sank into the river the color of blood, at once a wind sprang up and covered the sky with black, yellow, and green clouds the size of whales, which moved across the face of the moon. The river was covered with foam, and against the landing the boats strained in the waves and strained again. River and bluff gave off alike a leaf-green light, and from the water's edge the red torches lining the Landing-under-the-Hill and climbing the bluff to the town stirred and blew to the left and right. There were sounds of rushing and flying, from the flourish of carriages hurrying through the streets after dark, from the bellowing throats of the flatboatmen, and from the wilderness itself, which lifted and drew itself in the wind, and pressed its savage breath even closer to the little galleries of Rodney, and caused a bell to turn over in one of the steeples, and shook the fort and dropped a tree over the racetrack.

Another book that celebrates the dark and light sides of life with terror and wonder and thanksgiving is *Dandelion Wine* by Ray Bradbury. It too is a book I must read every year; it too drives the drizzly November out of my soul. *Dandelion Wine* is about the experiences of a boy's twelfth summer, experiences that teach him that death

Marilyn Arnold

and loss are corollaries to life and discovery. It is also about people, the people who live in Douglas Spaulding's house and Grandma's house and a dozen other houses in Green Town, Illinois, in the summer of 1929. There is Helen Loomis, who in her nineties embarks on a compelling intellectual companionship with a man half her age, a companionship doomed to bow too soon to death. There is Lavinia Nebbs, who journeys late at night through the frightening ravine only to find the murderous "Lonely One" has invaded the sanctity of her own home. There is Colonel Freeleigh, the "Time Machine," who, confined to his bed, takes the neighbor boys with him into the past to live again the Battle of Bull Run and the shooting of Ching Ling Soo. There is Leo Auffmann, who builds a Happiness Machine only to discover that the true happiness machine is his home and family. There is Mrs. Bentley, who has spent her life saving mementos from the past and is finally taught by children to live in the present. Perhaps most memorable of all is Great-grandma, who, at age ninety-four, decides that she wants to quit while life's game is still fun. This is the kind of woman she is:

She was a woman with a broom or a dustpan or a washrag or a mixing spoon in her hand. You saw her cutting piecrust in the morning, humming to it, or you saw her setting out the baked pies at noon or taking them in, cool, at dusk. She rang porcelain cups like a Swiss bell ringer, to their place. She glided through the halls as steadily as a vacuum machine, seeking, finding, and setting to rights. She made mirrors of every window, to catch the sun. She strolled but twice through any garden, trowel in hand, and the flowers raised their quivering fires upon the warm air in her wake. She slept quietly and turned no more than three times in a night, as relaxed as a white glove to which, at dawn, a brisk hand will return. Waking, she touched people like pictures, to set their frames straight. . . .

Now it was as if a huge sum in arithmetic were finally drawing to an end. She had stuffed turkeys, chickens, squabs, gentlemen, and boys. She had washed ceilings, walls, invalids, and children. She had laid linoleum, repaired bicycles, wound clocks, stoked furnaces, swabbed iodine on ten thousand grievous wounds. Her hands had flown all around about and down, gentling this, holding that, throwing baseballs, swinging bright croquet mallets, seeding black earth, or fixing covers over dumplings, ragouts, and children wildly strewn by slumber. She had pulled down shades, pinched out candles, turned switches, and—grown old. Looking back on thirty billions of things started, carried, finished and done, it all summed up, totaled out; the last decimal was placed, the final zero swung into line. Now, chalk in hand, she stood back from life a silent hour before reaching for the eraser.

Ready now for the one experience she has not yet tasted, death, Great-grandma takes to her bed and calls the family to her side one by one. Perhaps my favorite lines in the whole book occur when twelve-year-old Douglas approaches her bed. His first troubled question to the dying woman is, "Grandma, who'll shingle the roof next spring?" Douglas remembers that "every April for as far back as there were calendars, you thought you heard woodpeckers tapping the housetop. But no, it was Great-grandma somehow transported, singing, pounding nails, replacing shingles, high in the sky!" Great-grandma's whispered reply to Douglas is very important: "Douglas, . . . don't ever let anyone do the shingles unless it's fun for them. . . . Look around come April, and say, 'Who'd like to fix the roof?' And whichever face lights up is the face you want, Douglas. Because up there on that roof you can see the whole town going toward the country and the country going toward the edge of the earth, and the river shining, and the morning lake, and the birds on the trees down under you, and the best of the wind all around above. Any one of those should be enough to make a person climb a weather vane some spring sunrise. It's a powerful hour, if you give it half a chance. . . ."

I might say of books what Great-grandma said of spring sunrises. They are powerful, if you give them half a chance. Endless numbers of books have touched my life in remarkable ways. We sometimes speak of books as means for escaping life temporarily, but for me a worthy book is not so much an escape as it is a plunge into the very heart of life. Life is the very stuff of which books are made. A book is not an escape from experience; it is experience. I have had many great teachers in my life, and some of the best of them have been books.

Marilyn Arnold received her bachelor's and master's degrees from Brigham Young University and a Ph.D. from the University of Wisconsin. A former assistant to the president at BYU, she is currently associate professor of English. In the Church she has been chairman of the Relief Society Cultural Refinement Curriculum Committee and is now a member of the Sunday School general board. She has published extensively in professional journals as well as Church publications.

THE JOYS OF BEING ORGANIZED

Nancy Marriott

Look to this day!
For it is life, the very life of life.
In its brief course
Lie all the verities and realities of your existence:
The bliss of growth;
The glory of action;
The splendor of achievement;
For yesterday is but a dream,
And tomorrow is only a vision;
But today, well lived, makes every yesterday a dream of happi-
*   ness,*
And every tomorrow a vision of hope.
Look well, therefore, to this day!
Such is the salutation to the dawn.

This beautiful poem by the Indian dramatist Kalidasa reminds us how precious and important each day should be to us. Each day brings opportunities for happiness, achievement, and joy, or, conversely, for discouragement, frustration, and disappointment. Truly, all our memories and hopes center on our making the most of our todays.

I believe that the key to getting the most out of the day, the cornerstone of success, self-esteem, and joy, is organization. Effective organization can eliminate so many of the pressures and misunderstandings of everyday life. Our family has learned, through various experiences with planning dances, roadshows, projects, and parties, that personal preparation can bring peace of mind and a greater access to the spirit of the Lord, while organization on a group level can promote feelings of brotherhood and achievement.

"Organize yourselves," the Lord commands; "prepare every needful thing; and establish a house, even a house of prayer, a house of fasting, a house of faith, a house of learning, a house of glory, a house of order, a house of God." (D&C 88:119.) What a divine challenge!

I find that any increase in responsibility seems to be accompanied by an increased need for organization. I use several devices to help me keep track of where I'm headed, what I want to accomplish, and how I'm going to make it.

The first thing I do is set goals. When I know which direction I'm going in, it's much easier to perceive ways to chart the course.

Next, I make a list of everything I need to get done in order to accomplish my goals. I put stars by the things that are most important. This involves thinking ahead as much as possible; many a well-laid plan has been thwarted by some appointment or obligation remembered at the last minute. It helps to keep a calendar upon which all appointments are listed so that a quick glance will reveal any potential conflicts.

I also make notes for myself and for other family members. It seems to cement something in the mind when time is taken to write it down. And the paper generally has a better memory than I do.

Perhaps the most important thing to remember in organizing our lives is not to get discouraged. Conflicts will inevitably arise from time to time and play havoc with our carefully laid-out schedules. Plans may not work the way we want them to. But if we are flexible and optimistic, these temporary setbacks need not keep us from reaching our ultimate goals. Elder Marvin J. Ashton has said, "We have not failed until we have quit trying." If one approach does not work, there might be another one that will.

One effective way of fighting discouragement is to remember its source: Satan. Satan has a whole catalog of convincing reasons why we should not put forth our best efforts. He knows that we draw closer to God and increase our capacities for service when we organize our priorities, so he will do everything in his power to keep us from progressing.

Actually, Satan's job is not always as difficult as it should be. We often stall our own progress because of our fears. It takes effort to grow. Stretching, as we find when we overtax an underworked muscle, can be painful. We've all experienced the frustrations of taking over a new position, learning an unfamiliar skill, or being placed in a situation where we have to work something back and forth and in and out before it comes out right. It's not easy! But the self-esteem and growth that come through actually working through and rising above the difficulties provide a lasting sense of joy.

Once when I was playing tennis I swung my racket around quickly to prepare for a backhand shot. I found myself losing control as the racket slipped from my grasp and flew into the air. *I've got to get a better grip,* I told myself, *and pay more attention to what I'm doing.* Then it struck me that we must do the same thing in gaining control of our lives: we have to pay attention to the circumstances surrounding us and get a good grip on ourselves. Then we will be less likely to lose our hold on the day, the hour, the week, or the life.

Although our first organizational responsibilities involve our own lives, we have many opportunities to extend these skills to larger groups. The basic procedures are similar: we start by setting goals. It is important for several reasons to allow for everyone's input in this goal-setting stage. First, people are more likely to cooperate, to feel motivated, when they have helped set the goals. These goals become the team's goals rather than the leader's goals, and everyone has a personal investment in them.

Second, communication is easier when everyone has a

basic idea of what a project is designed to accomplish. Things run much more smoothly when everyone is headed in the same direction to begin with. Many clashes, miscommunications, and aggravations can be avoided by beginning an undertaking this way.

Finally, a variety of input will generate a variety of ways to accomplish the goals. It is important to have alternative ideas available in case something goes wrong with the initial plans. Again, frustration can be averted by flexibility, and flexibility becomes easier when many alternatives are available.

Once the initial goals have been outlined, a time frame needs to be set for accomplishing them. Knowing the time involved and getting started early can eliminate many last-minute disasters. Kinks and potential problems can be observed early, when the pressure is less intense. Also, group members can fit the goals more comfortably into their schedules with other activities.

Now the work begins: putting the steps of the plan into operation. At this point it becomes very important to engender enthusiasm among the group members. This excitement is highly contagious and can really help a project move along. I discovered this one fall as I planted daffodil bulbs with my children. Having four daughters has been a marvelous experience for many reasons, but chief among these is watching the development of their different personalities and seeing these personalities interact with each other. Some of the girls were very excited about our daffodil project; others were not. But the enthusiasm of the former soon spread to the less enthusiastic, and before I knew it the bulbs were almost all in the ground.

Certainly proper organization in the early stages of the project allows this carrying-out stage to be much more joyous. When the frustrations and pressures have been eased by effective planning, there is more time and energy available for enthusiasm and creativity. This is one of the great joys of organization: the fulfillment that comes from a job well done.

All this is not to say, however, that organization can eliminate discouragement entirely. Things still do—and always will—go wrong. Homework assignments, sports team practices, church meetings, music lessons, home teaching: any number of activities may arise to conflict with the desired schedule. But the leader's dedication and willingness to work around these barriers can weld the group together into a motivated, enthusiastic unit.

For example, our family was once asked to participate in a musical performance at the Church's information center in Washington, D.C. Working rehearsal times around seminary, after-school sports, homework assignments, and "sacrificed" free time required self-discipline and careful time budgeting. All of us had to better organize our individual and group time to pull together this missionary effort. Rising earlier in the morning, practicing individual parts before joining together as a unit, and other such things helped demonstrate to our young daughters that sacrifices come in different packages. The experience they gained in exercising tolerance and patience will aid them later as they strive to organize their own lives. And the sacrifices they made for the sake of the performance will help prepare them for the times ahead when greater sacrifices will be required.

Certainly the joys we felt from seeing the success of our efforts as a family team helped erase all memory of the discouragements we had encountered along the way. Some other things that might help keep a group project from ending in disillusionment are: (1) avoiding criticism of group members, (2) being willing to learn from mistakes, and (3) keeping long-range goals in mind.

Nothing can kill enthusiasm and initiative faster than excessive criticism. Certainly mistakes must be dealt with, but little is accomplished if group members are made to feel inadequate or unqualified. Suggestions should be made in a positive, strengthening manner. When each member senses that he is a vital part of the group and its achievements, negative competition is decreased and self-esteem enhanced.

It's not easy to step back and let an underachiever reap the benefits of our hard work, or to help an individual with no reward in mind, but it becomes easier when we remember the sweet promise of the scriptures: "Inasmuch as ye have done it unto one of the least of these my brethren, ye have done it unto me." (Matthew 25:40.)

Being human, we will inevitably make mistakes. We can use our mistakes as excuses not to go on with the work, or we can view them as learning experiences and accept the lessons they may offer. The latter requires a humble, teachable attitude, for only the humble will admit their mistakes, and only the teachable will learn from them. No one likes to fail, but failure need never occur if mistakes are approached with an optimistic attitude and a sincere effort to improve. Facing the problem immediately and courageously can prevent it from getting worse or from generating other problems.

The Lord never promised us that we would always succeed. Instead, he offered us the opportunity to accept challenges that stretch and develop us. Keeping in mind our long-range goals puts these challenges into perspective. Many times our difficulties are not nearly so traumatic as we make them out to be. Learning to look at them objectively and to see how they fit into the long-range scheme of things may help shrink them to their proper proportions.

Ultimately, all our earthly goals culminate in our eternal goals. How well we handle our challenges in this life may determine the opportunities we will have to grow and develop in the next. Eternal progression is the whole purpose of the plan of salvation, and the ability to organize plays a key role, for God's house is a house of order.

God wants us to have joy. It is one of the primary purposes of our existence: "Men are, that they might have joy." (2 Nephi 2:25.) We learned of this great joy in our premortal existence where, at the prospect of coming here to earth to gain a body of flesh and bones and to use our free agency during this probationary time, "all the sons of God shouted for joy." (Job 38:7.) By organizing our lives, we can have more time to feel the joy, more perceptivity to recognize the joy, and more capacity for sharing the joy.

Nancy Peery Marriott received a bachelor's degree from the University of Utah, and attended the International Interior Design School in Washington, D.C., and Longy School of Music in Boston. She has been active in auxiliaries of the Church, and has also achieved recognition in art and music. In 1976 she was named one of the Outstanding Young Women of America. She and her husband, Richard Edwin Marriott, and their four daughters reside in Washington, D.C.

THE JOYS OF WORK

Lucile C. Reading

The past few years friends have often asked, "Lucile, why don't you stop working so hard and do what you want for a change?" I am not being Pollyannaish when I reply, "Why, I'm doing just what I want—working hard. And I'm being blessed beyond my deserving."

Perhaps my feelings are similar to those of Thomas A. Edison when his wife complained that he worked too hard and needed a rest. "You must forget about work and go on a vacation," she declared.

"But where would I go?" he asked.

Her reply was simple. "Just decide where you'd rather be than anywhere else on earth, and then go there."

"Very well," promised Edison. "I will go there tomorrow."

And the next morning he went back to work in his laboratory.

Those many years ago when I was a child, I grew up as one of the middle children of a large family whose number often swelled to include three or four relatives or friends who needed a temporary or permanent home. It was unthinkable that any of the conglomerate group would do less than the allotted fair share of work, and the highest of family praise was to be dubbed "a hard worker."

This commendation implied that the person so referred to did not noticeably shirk any assigned task and accepted responsibility without obvious complaint. The title was always associated with physical labor, just as the term *hard work* is usually so associated in the minds of many people today.

The dictionary definition of work is much broader: "activity in which one exerts strength or faculties to do or perform something. Sustained physical or mental effort to overcome obstacles and achieve an objective or result."

Over the years I have learned that physical work is often less difficult than work that involves intangible qualities not necessarily equated with manual strength.

It is also intriguing to consider the difference between work and *hard* work, since I see no definite line that separates the two. Does the word *work* without the qualifying adjective imply routine, boring, minimal, grudging, mechanical, halfhearted, or anything-to-get-by labor? Is hard work that which is done earnestly, gladly, creatively, steadily, enthusiastically, and gratefully? Does the difference depend on the worker doing everything possible to accomplish a given task, going beyond the expected or ordinary? Is it work that is done with such wholehearted giving of self that a worker so employed can both lose and find himself in it? My answers would be *yes*, for that is how I work, and therein I find joy.

My husband made an interesting observation some years ago that might explain my appellation of a hard worker. At the time I was volunteering service to a state health organization. One evening I was greatly concerned about a problem in connection with a patient.

"Why are you so upset?" he asked.

"Well," I replied, "because I'm beginning to understand what this program is all about and how important it is to people, so I'm really becoming involved in it."

He smiled in a knowing way. "I don't think it's entirely that," he countered. "It's probably because you don't get lightly involved in whatever you do; you always become obsessed with it."

While this is, of course, some exaggeration (and he was sometimes given to such, especially with regard to his wife), I do become deeply involved and find great joy in whatever I am doing. Complete involvement is the only way I know how to work, certainly the only joyous way.

And the way in which one can grow. I have often observed that what is hard work at one period of life or under certain unpleasant circumstances becomes easier at another time. This could be because of Emerson's statement (often attributed to President Heber J. Grant): "That which we persist in doing becomes easier for us to do; not that the nature of the thing itself is changed, but our power to do is increased."

Not only does repetition usually make work easier, but new techniques are developed, a more efficient organization may result, or a fresh approach may be taken that gives the worker the added joy of viewing it no longer as a routine laborer, but from the exciting and satisfying point of view as a creator of something at least partially new.

Changing circumstances of personnel or place might also make hard work seem easier and more pleasant. Wholly different reasons for exerting extra effort provide greater stimulation and determination. I think often of the hard work and hardships undertaken by our early pioneers who, at such great sacrifice, left their homes and loved ones to take part in the gathering of the Saints in Zion. Their conviction and fervor not only motivated them to sacrifice ease and to travel under incredibly difficult conditions, but also made it possible for them to sing, "No toil nor labor fear, but with joy wend your way" as they journeyed.

I have learned that when I give myself freely and wholly and enthusiastically to do what I believe must be done to reach either a long- or short-range goal for myself or to help others, I receive one of the greatest of joys associated with and as a result of hard work—growth. Growth of mind and body and spirit. Even though there are some failures along the way, I still sense a certain growth, sometimes because of those very failures.

Buckminster Fuller, a designer and author, perceptively wrote, ". . . man always learns more. He cannot learn less." And in hard work there is always learning, always growth.

Ida M. Tarbell, author and editor, once wrote, "The most satisfying interest in my life, books and friends and beauty aside, is work—plain hard steady work." I can make the same assertion, although I would add to Miss Tarbell's exceptions the Church and my family. I have found hard work not only a most satisfying interest but also an absolute essential in my life, despite the fact that it sometimes carries with it disappointment, frustrations, failure, fatigue, and sacrifice. I have learned, too, that the more I am faced with these burdens that come in the package labeled "Hard Work," and the harder I have to work to overcome them, the more intense is the joy that comes through challenge and accomplishment, even though I might sight only signposts of progress along the way toward the ultimate goal.

In hard work I find escape from trivial annoyances, forgetfulness of heartache, relief from restlessness, the sweet healing of sorrow, comfort in times of disillusionment, gladness from knowing I can still work, excitement in meeting recurring challenges, and an ever-freshening delight in accomplishment, even though that accomplishment might seem small in the eyes of others.

It is exhilarating to awaken each morning knowing that there is hard work waiting for me, that there is something that must be done, and that someone thinks I can do it. Such knowledge gives me a sense of belonging to our wonderful working world and a feeling of self-worth. It is pleasurable to believe that someone needs me, that I can fulfill that need, and that no one else can do what I have to do—not because they are less capable, but because it is not their responsibility; it is most uniquely mine.

For a mother in a home, it is not always easy to sustain this cheerful view; but such vision for a woman whose role places her in a home is the only truism. No one else is the mother of her children, no one else is the wife of her husband, no one else is as needed in that particular home as she is, no one else can fill that need as well as she, and no one else could possibly know the joy that can be hers through her work!

Work comes in other guises to those who perform outside of the home. I know, because I've worked hard both in and outside of my home. I've found satisfying and joy-filled work through Church callings, in volunteer work in many fields, and in work that has met a financial necessity to help support a family or to maintain myself.

In all of these situations, one can pleasurably sense growth. As John Ruskin once wisely said, "The highest reward for man's toil is not what he gets for it but what he becomes by it." And regardless of our circumstances, we become happier and better through satisfying, mind- and body-stretching, spirit-lifting, and creative hard work.

In contemplation of writing my feelings about work, I've entertained some interesting questions I've never explored before in quite the same way:

Did God work hard in creating the world, or was the hard work done while planning and then delegating responsibility for its creation? He must have had a glorious sense of satisfaction when it was completed, because he tells us in Moses 2:31, "And I, God, saw everything that I had made, and, behold, all things which I had made were very good."

Is it hard work to keep the stars moving, every planet in its place, every eclipse right on the minute, the clouds regularly moving according to the air currents? Is it hard to keep living plants going through their assigned periods of growth—blossoming, dying, and then changing form to fertilize other plants? This is a working universe. How then can anyone justify idleness, or exert only the minimum effort in work that must be done?

Is the attitude we have toward work an extension of

our personal philosophy, indicating what we value, what motivations we have that drive us to work ever harder?

Is Satan working harder to tempt and try us than the Lord to strengthen and sustain us? But then, aren't we in all ways free agents and, therefore, responsible for how we work and how we live regardless of whoever and whatever seeks to influence us?

I believe that how I work is indicative of how I want to live—fully and joyously, regardless of circumstances. How I work is a reflection of my faith, my philosophy, my integrity, my ideals, and my commitments. I want to earn what I have, knowing that I must also earn whatever I may eventually become.

John A. Widtsoe declared, "The man who believes that he is born to find joy, but must win it by earning it, walks through life with head up and a steady fearless heart. To him labor brings joy."

This much I know: As long as life and ability endure, I shall be hard at work at something, doing some work somewhere that stretches my mind, challenges my body, and enriches my soul. I shall try to walk through what life remains to me with my head up and a steady fearless heart, for I know that in so doing I shall continue to find joy in working hard every blessed day.

Lucile C. Reading has been managing editor of the Friend *since 1970; previously she served as a counselor in the general Primary presidency. A graduate of Utah State University, she recently received the USU Distinguished Service Award. She is president of the Davis County (Utah) Board of Education and secretary of the Lakeview Hospital board; she has also served on the boards of the Primary Children's Medical Center, South Davis Community Hospital, USU Alumni Association, and South Davis Chamber of Commerce. She has two sons and five grandchildren.*

INDEX

Index